THE NEW YORK CALL MONEY MARKET

1837
ARTES
VERITAS
SCIENTIA
LIBRARY OF THE
UNIVERSITY OF MICHIGAN
TUEBOR
CIRCUMSPICE

THE NEW YORK CALL MONEY MARKET

By

BARTOW GRIFFISS

A DISSERTATION

SUBMITTED TO THE BOARD OF UNIVERSITY STUDIES OF THE JOHNS HOPKINS UNIVERSITY IN CONFORMITY WITH THE REQUIREMENTS FOR THE DEGREE OF DOCTOR OF PHILOSOPHY

THE RONALD PRESS COMPANY
NEW YORK

PREFACE

This study seeks to analyze the position which the New York call money market holds in the financial and economic structure of the country and to present an accurate description of its organization and operation.

While the call money market in New York is the chief source of funds for financing speculative purchases of securities, no one has seen fit to give a clear and full explanation of its activities. Those closely connected with it have a tendency to take for granted that it is generally known and appreciated by the public. As a matter of fact, however, the public is very imperfectly informed on the subject. Widely conflicting views are current not merely as to the organization and operation of the market but even as to its nature and value. Many persons, pointing to the high rates of interest paid on call loans when money market conditions are stringent, assert that the call market is under the control of a small coterie of Wall Street bankers who exercise such control for their own profit. Some regard this market as an inherently evil institution, which should if possible be eliminated.

In this study, accordingly, the object has been to give an unbiased account of the organization and functioning of the call money market, to dispel misconceptions as to its nature, and to point out any weaknesses in the system which appear to demand modification.

Most of the material has been obtained at first hand, through interviews with men who have intimate knowledge of the money market as lenders or borrowers of call funds—that is to say, with brokers and others connected with the New York Stock Exchange and also with bankers. Without the aid of these men this material would not have been available. Special acknowledgment is to be made in this connection to Edward Meeker, Economist of the New York Stock Exchange; Samuel Streit, member of the New York Stock Exchange and President of its Stock Clearing Corporation; Benjamin Strong, Governor of the Federal Reserve Bank of New York; E. R. Kenzel, Deputy Governor; Paul Warburg, Chairman of the Board of the International Acceptance Corporation; and Wallace Jackson, formerly of Hartman Co., Brokers, of Baltimore.

For inspiration and helpful criticism throughout the undertaking the author is very greatly indebted to Professors Jacob H. Hollander and George E. Barnett of Johns Hopkins University.

Bartow Griffiss

Pittsburgh, Pa.
January 15, 1925.

INTRODUCTORY NOTE

One of the least understood features of the American money market is that ordinarily referred to as "the call money rate." Insufficiently described and imperfectly analyzed in economic textbooks, the current impression is a mixture of vagueness and error. It is high time that there should be available for those who study, as well as for those who engage in the operations of the money market, a clear account of this mechanism and of the notable changes which it has undergone in the past ten years.

The present essay undertakes to perform this service. It is marked by entire objectivity in approach and presumable accuracy in treatment. Concerned in the main with orderly description, the essay touches in the closing sections upon the wider reaches of the subject. Here there is room for further laborious research. With the foreground cleared, we may expect that the author will press his inquiry into this uncleared zone with the same diligence and fidelity that distinguish the present survey.

JACOB H. HOLLANDER

The Johns Hopkins University,
January 20, 1925.

CONTENTS

THE NEW YORK CALL MONEY MARKET

CHAPTER I

ELEMENTARY CONCEPTS

Time Loans and Call Loans.—The purpose of this chapter is to explain the fundamental principles and definitions which are connected with call loans as they are made in the New York money market. Discussion of those factors which affect call loans at different times as results of changes in the organization of the money market will be left for later discussion.

If security collateral loans are classified as to their maturity, we find that there are two kinds: first, time loans, and, secondly, what are known as call or demand loans. The time loan is made for some definite length of time, ranging generally from thirty to ninety days. The rate of interest which the borrowers is to pay the lender for the use of this money is agreed upon beforehand so that there is no change in the interest rate during the life of the loan. These loans are made by merchants for financing the purchase of goods, by manufacturers for the purchase of raw materials, by farmers for the financing of their crops and for other needs of circulating capital. Of course some are made for consumption loans, but most are made with the purpose of facilitating production.

The other kind of security loan is the call or the demand loan. The difference in the maturity of the call loan and the time loan is that, whereas the latter runs for some such period as noted above, the call loan runs, theoretically, only for a day. A call loan may be extended for another day, and so on indefinitely, but its specific duration, at any time, is only a single day. The interest rate on a call loan is likely to change from day to day. The first interest rate may be at one figure, and then the next day or the day after, there may be a decided change in the rate. These changes in the interest rates on call loans have led to much of the discussion in regard to them.

There is no difference in the kind of collateral which may be used in either type of loan; either may be secured by stocks, bonds, or short-term paper in the form of acceptances, in fact by any sort of security which the lender is willing to accept. But the majority of the call loans are made with stocks and bonds as security.

Reasons for Growth of New York Call Money Market.—The call loan market in New York is a result of two chief factors:

1. The daily settlement system which is used by the New York Stock Exchange.
2. The nature of the banking system prior to 1914.

The use of the daily settlement means that every broker who is buying and selling upon the Stock Exchange must settle all his accounts resulting from each day's business so that the next day he starts with his accounts entirely balanced in regard to business previously transacted. Most sales of securities made on the Exchange are made for delivery and payment on the following full business day. This system of settlements requires brokers who buy stocks upon margin to obtain credit which will vary from one day to the next with any variations which take place in the amount of securities they have bought and are holding on margin. Most of the securities which are purchased upon margin are bought not for the brokers themselves but for their various customers who give them orders to buy these stocks or bonds. But whether the broker buys stocks on margin for himself or for his customer, it is always the broker's business to arrange the call loan to finance the transaction. If the purchase is made in behalf of the customer of a broker, then the transaction is financed in the following way: The broker requires the customer to furnish about twenty per cent of the total amount of money needed to purchase the securities desired, and then arranges with a lender to give him a loan for the other eighty per cent of the amount of money needed. At the same time the lender is given either the securities bought as collateral against the loan, or else some other collateral which is satisfactory to him. This question of collateral will be considered at greater length later, the purpose here being merely to show the way in which the necessity of obtaining call loans arises.

The second important factor was the nature of the banking system prior to the enactment of the Federal Reserve Act in 1913, and the installation of our new banking system in the following year. Under the older banking system, bankers all over the country were in great need of an absolutely liquid form of investment in which they could place funds which they could count as a secondary reserve. The money market in New York furnished them this needed facility in the form of loans which could be terminated at any time, thereby releasing the money for other uses. As there was no broad discount market, it was not possible for the banks to invest their funds in short-time commercial paper. This kind of paper was not widely used in this country, and has only come into any wide use since the inauguration of the federal reserve system. Rather than have funds lie idle in the vaults of banks when there was no use for them at home, the bankers would send them to New York, where they would draw a certain return and could be recalled at any time.

The banking system and the New York money market developed together and were interdependent. After New York established its supremacy as the financial center of the country, no other city could compete as a money market and as a place for the flotation of new corporate issues. There was some early competition from the other cities of the Atlantic Seaboard, but New York soon outstripped them all, and since an early date has been supreme as the money center of this country.

Importance of the New York Money Market.— The New York money market would not have such great importance as a financial institution if it financed only those stock transactions which originate in New York City, but such is not the case. Stocks which are sold on the New York Stock Exchange are purchased by different brokerage houses all over the country for customers of these houses, and all transactions in which stocks are bought on margin are financed in the New York money market. If, for example, a man in Baltimore wished to purchase a hundred shares of United States Steel Common on a margin of twenty per cent, he would go to the brokerage house in Baltimore where he deals and give them an order to purchase this stock for him on the New York Stock Exchange. The Baltimore brokerage firm then telegraphs its representative in New York, which is a firm able to purchase this stock upon the New York Exchange, and orders the stock to be purchased and held for their account. As a result the New York broker executes the order and buys one hundred shares of United States Steel Common, charging this amount to the account of the broker in Baltimore from whom he has received the order. The loan for the remaining eighty per cent of the purchase price is arranged by the New York broker and the stock bought is given as collateral against the loan, or else some other satisfactory collateral is used to secure the loan, in the same way as though the stock was purchased by a man in New York. Consequently, no matter where throughout the country the purchasers of New York securities may be, the whole transaction takes place in New York, and the money used to finance all deals of this type is drawn from the money market in New York City. The stock certificate never leaves New York at all, but is held there as security for the loan which has been made for the balance of the purchase price of the stock. When the customer who has purchased the hundred shares of United States Steel Common desires to sell again, he goes to his broker in Baltimore and gives him an order to sell out the stock. The Baltimore broker again transmits the order to the representative in New York and the New York broker sells the hundred shares, paying off the loan contracted at the time of the purchase with the proceeds of the sale. The cash balance resulting from this sale is then paid by the Baltimore broker to his customer and the two brokerage houses settle up the charges at the end of the month.

In actual practice, however, the call loan unit of $100,000 is larger than the average customer's transaction of one hundred shares, which would ordinarily amount to about $10,000. Hence the broker does not, in fact, usually liquidate an entire loan to obtain a hundred share certificate, but he will substitute other securities as collateral for the loan to take the place of those which he must withdraw. The total amount of the loans which an individual broker has does not, in ordinary times, vary a great deal, for there is a constant stream of new purchasers who are coming to take the place of those who wish to sell their holdings.

A further demand for call loans arises on the part of syndicates who use collateral loans to carry new security issues in the process of distribution. These issues are generally put out at a time when the money market is well supplied with funds, and there is plenty of money available at low rates of interest. These call loans, which arise out of the financing of new issues, have a stabilizing effect upon the money market, and lessen the variations in the demand for funds.

Three Different Call Money Markets in New York City.—There are in reality three distinct markets for call loans in New York City, and each one may be treated as a separate market in which loans are differently made:

The money broker.
The banks.
The New York Stock Exchange.

The money broker makes it his business to loan money; some, perhaps, loan on call and some in time loans. When anyone wishes to secure a call loan he may arrange with one of these money brokers to lend him the money. The rate of interest will generally coincide with the current rate of interest being charged for such loans upon the Stock Exchange, but there is no definite rule in this matter, and there may be a variation between the rate which is charged by the broker and the current rate, according to the arrangements which are made between the broker and the borrower. The money lender is an intermediary who places the loans for banks or corporations who wish to loan money on call. Then he secures loans for borrowing brokers and others who wish to obtain such loans. Each money broker is thus a small money market in himself, really a distributing agency for credit, securing funds from those who have little temporary use for them and lending to those who are in need of temporary funds.

The second market for call loans is composed of banks. In this case the customer of a bank will arrange with his bank to lend him money on call rather than resort to a broker or the Stock Exchange. The rate of interest which is charged upon loans made directly through a bank sometimes coincides with the rate charged upon the Stock Exchange, and at other times there may be a difference between the two. It often happens that customers make loans with their bank with certain provisions which do not exist in the loans made upon the Exchange. For example there may be the provision in a loan which is made between the bank and its customer, that the rate of interest will not rise above a certain rate, and will not fall below a certain rate. Both parties are thus assured that there will not be any great variation in the rate even if the market rate fluctuates widely. The borrower is assured that he will not have to pay more than the maximum, and the bank is assured that it will not get less than the minimum rate decided upon for the loan. As these rates are given no publicity, it is not possible to tell the exact rate at which these loans are being made. In these loans there is a limitation of the risk which the parties to the loans must otherwise necessarily run if there is the chance of large variations in the rate. Both the lender and the borrower feel more secure, and there is not so much speculation as there must be in regard to loans which are often made in the Exchange, where there is no certainty as to just what the rate of interest will be on a loan if there should be a sudden shortage of funds, as often occurred under the National Banking system.

There is a sharp contrast in this matter of publicity between the loans which are made on the Stock Exchange and those which are made in the other two markets. In the former the rates are published daily. Although there is often some publication of rates for call loans made outside the Exchange, still these rates are not authentic. Many banks prefer to loan directly to their customers, because here there exists the relationship of lender and borrower accompanied with some personal acquaintance and knowledge which is lacking in those loans which are made on the Exchange. When loans are made on the floor of the Exchange the borrower and the lender do not know each other, and as a result neither is able to select the party with whom he is going to deal. Furthermore, it is far easier in most cases for banks to make loans to customers, as there is no difficulty about securing the satisfactory collateral and passing upon it, whereas this process often necessitates much running back and forth between the lender and the borrower, when a loan is placed on the Exchange.

The third market for call loans is the money market on the New York Stock Exchange, the only one of its kind in the country. It is the one with which we are most intimately concerned. Here money is borrowed and loaned as any other commodity might be exchanged in an open market for the purpose. Loans are here made under conditions entirely different from those in either of the other markets for call loans. One of the greatest points of difference arises from the fact that, when loans are made in the money market of the Stock Exchange, the lenders are not, in most cases, able to pick out the borrowers of their funds nor are borrowers able to tell by whom the funds they receive are loaned. The reason for this is that only members of the Stock Exchange can transact business upon the floor of the Exchange. As a result, any money to be loaned in this way, which is not owned by a member of the Exchange, must be loaned indirectly through some member.

Sources of the Funds for Call Loans.—The sources of the money loaned upon the Stock Exchange floor in the form of call loans are, in the main, the funds of three different kinds of business organizations:

1. Money brokers and other brokers who lend money on call.
2. Large corporations.
3. Banks, both inside and outside of New York City.

Organizations of the first class, the brokerage houses, may themselves lend their funds upon the money market in the Stock Exchange, providing they are members of the Exchange. Organizations of the second and third classes, which include all corporations and banks, cannot lend their money directly upon the floor of the Exchange, but must lend it through some broker who is a member. Corporations are periodic lenders and enter the market only when they have surplus funds for which they have no immediate use in their own enterprises. They frequently lend on the money market funds which are being accumulated for some particular purpose, such as the payment of dividends, and in these cases it is very convenient to be able to place these funds in a liquid form of investment which will afford a fair rate of return. As a result of this practice of corporations, it is apparent that there will be a larger amount of money from this source when the corporations are getting prepared for large dividend payments. Then there will be a withdrawal of funds when these payments fall due. Even if the corporations do not directly lend their funds on the Exchange, they may have them deposited in some bank which will lend the funds in the Call Money Market. This would have the same effect when it became necessary to withdraw these funds for other purposes.

Money brokers are always lending money in call loans, as this is a part of their regular business. Other brokers may lend funds at odd times, but as a rule it is not their own money. Banks must loan their money through some broker who is a member of the Exchange; consequently, various New York banks, which are in the habit of investing part of their funds in this way, have an arrangement with some particular broker upon the floor to make these loans for them. The broker does not charge the bank any commission for this service, but he is generally favored by the bank in the securing of time loans in return for his services. In fact he is generally a broker who has large dealings with the bank in other matters, and may be one of its largest customers.

All banks which loan on the Exchange may be divided into two classes according to whether they are New York City banks or out-of-town banks. The loans of the New York banks are known as "loans for their own account," while funds of out-of-town banks which are invested in call loans are known as "loans for the account of correspondents." Just as all banks in New York City must lend their money on the Stock Exchange through a broker, so all out-of-town banks must make their loans through some New York bank with whom they have an account. These New York banks with whom they have accounts are known as the New York correspondents of the out-of-town banks, and they act as their bankers for all business which is transacted in New York and which requires a bank there. No charge is made by the New York banks for investing this out-of-town money in call loans, but the out-of-town bank is expected and required to keep a balance in the New York bank in order to have this service performed. There is no definite and universally required proportion which must exist between this balance and the amount of loans made for the account of correspondents, but the New York bank will not allow the out-of-town bank to reduce its balance below a certain point and at the same time greatly increase the amount of money lent on the Exchange. There is generally a certain amount of balance which these out-of-town banks must keep in New York to meet their obligations there, and this must be kept irrespective of whether they lend money on call or not. The reason why the New York banks require this balance to be kept is that their sole source of profit with their out-of-town correspondents results from the money which they may be able to make from these funds which are deposited with them. A low rate of interest is paid on these balances, averaging about two per cent or a little higher. The low rate of interest gives the New York bank an opportunity to make use of the deposits of the out-of-town banks in lending these funds. Their profits depend upon the difference in the return which they get for the money and the amount which they must pay the out-of-town bank.

The Two Call Money Rates.—There are two rates of interest on call loans which always exist in the money market on the Stock Exchange. One rate is known as the market rate for money, and this is the rate at which new loans may be made at any time during the business day. The other rate is the renewal rate for call loans and this is the rate at which old call loans made before the current business day will be renewed for the day. All new loans are made at the market rate for one day only, and then if they last longer than a day they are generally renewed at the renewal rate. It will be seen that it is not necessary for all loans to follow the renewal rate after the first day they are made, but for the present we may take this as a general assumption. The result of the fact that the loans are made at the market rate for only one day is that about 95 per cent of the loans are not governed by the market rate, but a very large percentage of them follow the renewal rate. Furthermore, as the market rate is very indefinite, representing perhaps one or two small loans which have been made at that particular rate, it does not always mean a great deal. The renewal rate, however, may be taken as the rate at which most of the call loans stand. Here it may be noted that not all call loans stand for merely a day or two and then terminate; there is one example of a call loan standing for more than twelve years.

Method of Termination of Call Loans.—The call loan may be terminated in either of two ways: the lender may notify the borrower that his loan is called, with the result that the borrower must pay off the loan and the interest that day, or the borrower may inform the lender that he intends to pay off his loan. The reason that the lender calls the loan is generally that he needs the funds, thus invested, for some other purpose, while the reason that the borrower pays off the loan is that the transactions which necessitated this loan have been completed. If the loan was made for the purpose of holding securities which have been bought and held, then the securities have probably been sold again; and if it was made for the flotation of a new issue of securities, then the need of funds for this purpose no longer exists because the flotation has been completed. In order that neither lenders nor borrowers will be embarrassed by having a large percentage of these terminated or called at any one time it is customary for both lenders and borrowers to use a diversification of risk. Consequently, if a bank has half a million dollars to lend it will endeavor not to lend this whole amount to the same borrower, but to divide the amount between several borrowers, thus lessening the possibility of the whole amount of money becoming idle at one time, as would be the case if it were all in one loan which would be paid off at the time of its termination.

The hours of operation of the money market of the Stock Exchange are the same as those of transactions in stocks, and business begins at ten o'clock in the morning and ends at three in the afternoon. It is obvious that if lenders began calling their loans about two o'clock in the afternoon, there would soon develop a mad rush of borrowers to get these loans, which were thus called, placed with other lenders. The chance of any trouble of this sort has been obviated by the operation of an unwritten, but universally observed law of the Stock Exchange forbidding the calling of any loan after twelve-fifteen. As a result of this law, all brokers know that if their loans are not called up to this time, they will not be called until the next day. On the other hand it is not customary for brokers to terminate their loans at a late hour of the day, although there is no law or practice that there may not be the payment of a loan after twelve-fifteen.

The Security Collateral.—In normal times call loans usually amount to about 60 per cent and time loans to about 40 per cent of the total amount of outstanding security collateral loans. This ratio may change at different times. In dull periods of business the proportion of call loans will be diminished, while in periods of business activity and speculation, call loans may form nearly 75 per cent of the total amount of security collateral loans. This does not mean that the actual amount of money which is invested in time loans increases in periods of business depression, but rather that the relative amount which is invested at such times is larger than in periods of prosperity. The reason for this is that there is a greater variation in the demand for call loans than there is in the demand for time loans, and such things as speculation have more effect on demand loans than they have on time loans.

The total amount of money which is invested in call loans ranges from about half a billion dollars as a minimum to about a billion and a half dollars. When the Money Committee took control of the money market, at a period of great depression in the market, they found that the total amount of money invested in call loans was a little over four hundred millions of dollars. The peak of the loan account was reached in the period of speculation following the World War, when the volume of call loans reached 1,518 millions of dollars in the week of November seventh, 1919. In periods which are taken as being about as near normal as are possible to find, the amount of these loans averages between seven hundred and eight hundred millions of dollars.

The margin which the lender requires the borrower to furnish on call loans varies according to the type of the securities, the standing of the borrower, and the condition of the money market at the time that the loan is made. The ordinary amount of margin upon a so-called "regular loan," one which is made upon mixed collateral as security, is twenty-five per cent; the margin on loans based upon other collateral is ordinarily thirty per cent or more. By mixed collateral is meant that part of the securities are railroad stocks, or bonds, and part of them are industrial stocks, or bonds. The proportion existing in former years was two to one, with the preference for rails. Thus a regular loan was based upon securities comprising approximately 66-2/3 per cent railroad securities and 33-1/3 per cent industrial securities. It was not necessary for the proportions to be exactly two to one, but they approximated this ratio.

Recent Change in Attitude toward Collateral.—The feeling that rails were better collateral than industrials has changed a great deal in recent years, because of the far greater strength of most industrial stocks now in comparison with former years, especially those which have shown their stability for a number of years. They also now comprise a much larger proportion of the total securities on the Exchange than was the case formerly. This is due to the great growth which has taken place in the number of large corporations in industry. With the growth of these large corporations there has been an enormous increase in the amount of the capital necessary to finance them, and this has been secured by the issue of their securities which are sold on the Exchange. Some of the stocks of these industrial corporations are now considered to be nearly as safe as bonds; we have United States Steel as one of great strength. As a result of this change in attitude regarding industrials, a regular loan is now made upon security collateral comprising one-half rail securities, and one-half industrial securities. Below is given an example of an old regular loan and a new regular loan:

OLD REGULAR LOAN OF $100,000

Based upon mixed collateral; margin about 25%

400 Baltimore & Ohio	at	$ 40	$16,000
100 Union Pacific	at	138	13,800
200 N. Y. Chicago & St. Louis	at	81	16,200
200 Pennsylvania	at	46	9,200
200 Great Northern	at	80	16,000
200 United States Steel	at	107	21,400
300 Eastman Kodak	at	110	33,000
			$125,600

NEW REGULAR LOAN OF $100,000

Based upon mixed collateral; margin about 25%

200 Lehigh Valley	at	$ 64	$12,800
300 N. Y. Central	at	93	27,900
100 Central R. R. of N. J.	at	232	23,200
200 Beth. Steel	at	63	12,600
200 Amer. Tobacco	at	155	31,000
400 Kelly-Springfield	at	44	17,600
			$125,100

The margin required on a loan made upon securities which are composed entirely of rails is the same as that required on a regular loan. The margin required on a loan made upon all-industrial collateral is, however, higher than that required on either of these other two types, and the ordinary amount of margin is about thirty per cent. Ten years ago all-rail loans were quite common and all-industrial loans were very rare, whereas, now the reverse is the case, resulting in a large number of loans made upon all-industrial collateral.

Preferences of Lenders in Regard to Collateral.— The lender always has the privilege of forcing the borrower to substitute other collateral than that offered, in the event that he does not wish to accept some of the securities which the borrower has sent him. In this case the borrower must either change that part of the collateral which is undesirable, or his loan will be called. Lenders do not care to accept securities which fluctuate widely, and for this reason they require the borrower to change such securities or to put up a larger amount of them so that there will be a larger margin of safety. The ordinary broker only deals in round lots of stock, that is to say, lots of stock which are of one hundred shares or multiples of one hundred shares. If lots of less than a hundred shares are sold on the exchange they must be sold through odd lot dealers. These dealers mark their price from one-eighth to one-quarter of a per cent lower than the market price existing on the stock which they buy, and they sell stock at about the same amount above the market price. As a result of this fact round lots are more acceptable to the lender than odd lots, for they can be more easily disposed of than the latter. Consequently borrowers tend to make up collateral in the form of round lots so that the collateral will be in the most liquid form possible for sale if this should become necessary. Another type of security which is not favored by the lender is that which sells at a very high price, because, if there is a bad break in the market, these high-priced securities are very apt to lose most heavily.

Although lenders do not like these odd lots or widely fluctuating securities, they do, however, accept them. They often obtain more margin by marking down the prices of securities which have risen sharply. During the war, for example, Bethlehem Steel was always marked down a considerable amount below its extremely high selling price, which produced the same effect as requiring the borrower to put up additional collateral, or a larger margin to secure the loan. It should be borne in mind that marketability of the collateral is more desirable to the lender than is stability of price, as his interest in the securities which he accepts as collateral is as to whether he will be able to dispose of them readily on the market and get his money in event that the borrower is unable to pay off his loan when called. This is necessary in order that the call loan may be a highly liquid form of investment. If stability of price were the only thing considered by the lender, then he might find that the securities which he was holding for collateral were the most stable imaginable, but at the same time there might be no market for them and he would be unable to realize on them at the time when he needed the money tied up in the loan.

If the price of the securities held as collateral declines so that their total market value does not come up to the amount of the margin required by the lender, he will call upon the borrower to furnish him with additional collateral. Also if some of the securities later turn out to be undesirable, then he may get the borrower to substitute others. Borrowers nearly always give collateral which aggregates slightly more than the necessary margin, so that they will not be called upon to furnish more securities in the event that the market price upon some of these falls. Borrowing brokers as a rule, however, watch their loans as closely as lenders and they generally give the lender additional collateral even before they are called upon to do so; they take pride in the fact that the lender is not forced to call upon them. Frequently the borrower may wish to recover some particular security in the possession of the lender. The most frequent reason for this is that such security held by the lender has been sold by the borrower and that he wishes to obtain it for delivery to the purchaser. He is able to do this provided that he is able to substitute other security to take the place of the collateral withdrawn, which substitution must be acceptable to the lender.

Call Loans made on Acceptances as Collateral.—There remains one other entirely different kind of collateral which is now widely used in making call loans, namely, acceptances. Call loans made against acceptances generally command a lower rate of interest than those made against stock exchange securities. The preferential rate in regard to acceptances is a result of the policy of the federal reserve system, which allows acceptances to be rediscounted at the federal reserve banks by member banks. The federal reserve system does not, on the other hand, permit any such rediscount with regard to loans made against stock exchange securities, except those made against Liberty bonds and other obligations of the United States Government. Thus, if the borrower finds himself unable to pay off his loan when it is called, and the lending bank holds stock exchange securities other than the obligations of the United States Government as collateral against the loan, the only way that the bank can obtain the amount of the loan is to sell the securities in the open market. On the other hand, if the bank has acceptances as collateral and the borrower is not able to meet the loan when he is called upon to do so, then the bank is able to have the acceptances rediscounted at the federal reserve bank, and is not dependent upon the sale of the collateral upon the open market in order to obtain the funds thus tied up. As a result of the fact that the acceptances can be rediscounted, loans securied by them bear a rate of interest which is usually about one-half of one per cent lower than the rate of interest upon call loans made with Stock Exchange securities, except during periods when funds are very plentiful. Hence it is to the advantage of the borrower to give acceptances as collateral if it be possible. It is highly probable that the difference in the rate is not due to the fact that the loans made against acceptances are any better loans than those which are made against the other type of collateral, but more probably the difference is due to the fact that the Federal Reserve Board has tried to make the use of acceptances more general throughout the country. However there is a persistence of security collateral loans in competition with loans on acceptances, and it has appeared probable that there is not a great deal of difference in the relative liquidity of the two types of loans.

Arguments are given for and against both types of collateral. Those who are hostile to the use of stock exchange securities as collateral point to the one time in the history of the Stock Exchange when banks were not able to realize on these loans because of the fact that the Stock Exchange was closed for a time in 1914. The loans then became "frozen loans" which the banks had to hold. If they called them and the borrowers were not able to pay them off, then the bank would not have any market in which to dispose of the collateral. On the other hand, it is not such an unheard of thing for a bank to fail, as happened in 1920, and as very recently happened almost every week in the North-west. In that case the acceptances which were the obligations of these banks were no better than, and in many cases not as good as the stock exchange securities. The earliest time that the acceptances can be realized on in the case of the failure of a bank is after the affairs of the institution have been settled up, and then the amount that would be paid on these acceptances is uncertain and varies with the condition of the bank. In the crisis of 1920 no collateral loans were frozen, while many loans based on acceptances were frozen and the lenders were not able to obtain the funds thus tied up. It is also true that many banks, especially those in New York City, may not find it desirable to get back their funds invested in call loans if it is necessary for them to sell the securities held as collateral on the Stock Exchange. This is true because of the bad effects that would result in the consequent fall in the prices of securities which would be bound to accompany any large selling movement. Also this condition of the Stock Exchange would be likely to be reflected in business in general, and that would indirectly have bad results on the prosperity of the banks. Of course this argument holds true more for the banks in New York City than for country banks which do not feel that they are so directly concerned with the state of affairs in New York. Country banks are little likely to consider that the prosperity of the brokers on the Stock Exchange is their affair, as many of the people of other parts of the country are convinced that these brokers are a useless bunch of gamblers. The New York banks, however, will hesitate before they will call loans in a crisis, knowing that the result may well be serious financial embarrassment to their own customers. On the whole there seems to be little to choose between the two types of collateral used as security for call loans, and very little warrant for any difference in the rate of interest which they bear. The difference in interest rate seems to be due more to the policy of the Federal Reserve Board in regard to acceptances than to any inherent advantages in this type of collateral.

CHAPTER II

OPERATION OF THE CALL MONEY MARKET

Three Periods.—Three very different periods may be distinguished in the history of the money market of the New York Stock Exchange.

I. The first period covers the operation of the money market from its beginning up to the time of the entrance of the United States into the World War and the formation, in September 1917, of that organization known as the "Money Committee," which was a sub-committee of the Liberty Loan Committee.

II. The second period extends through the operation of the money market under the supervision and control of the Money Committee and ends with the termination of this control in January 1919.

III. The third and last period in the division extends from the relinquishment of control by the Money Committee up to the present time.

These three periods will be discussed in the order in which they fall historically.

First Period—Before September, 1917

The first period, that of the operation of the New York money market on the Stock Exchange up to the time of the entrance of the United States into the World War, is practically the same as that of the operation of the money market under the National Banking Act, because of the fact that the Federal Reserve System had very little chance to get into operation before the War.

The Money Post.—During this period in the history of the money market, all loans made upon the floor of the Stock Exchange were made at the "money post," which appeared like any stock trading post upon the floor and served the same purpose for transactions in call loans that a stock trading post serves for transactions in stocks. All brokers desirous of borrowing money on call, either for their own use or for others, would come to the "money post" and all the lending brokers would also bring their orders to loan funds to this same place. These two groups of brokers, composed of the borrowers and lenders, formed what was termed the "money crowd" upon the floor of the Exchange. The lending brokers not only brought the money of their own firms to lend, but also the funds of any bank in the city that was accustomed to do their call loan business through them.

Market Rate and Renewal Rate.—When the crowd had collected around the "money post," the borrowers called out their bids for money in the same way as a broker does who wishes to buy any particular stock at a stock trading post, and the lenders called out the rate of interest at which they were willing to loan their money, and also the quantity of money to be loaned at that particular rate. Loans were thus made by two members of the "money crowd" getting together, the one being a borrowing broker and the other a lender, and agreeing between themselves what the rate should be for the individual loan which was thus made. The first loan made after the market opened at ten o'clock in the morning established the market rate for loans. This rate was liable to fluctuate with any of the succeeding loans which might be made at some different rate of interest.

The fixture of the renewal rate for old loans was largely a matter of chance. After between two and three millions of dollars of new loans had been made, approximately the average of the rates of interest to be paid upon these loans was taken as the rate at which old loans should be renewed for that day. This renewal rate was, however, by no means universally followed by the banks or brokers lending money on the Exchange. Different banks and money brokers often established renewal rates at variance with each other. It was understood generally that if the borrower and lender did not get into communication with each other during the day, the rate of interest charged upon old loans remained the same. Thus, when there appeared a tendency for rates to drop, the borrower would try to get in touch with the lender in order to have the rate of interest charged upon his loan reduced, and when, on the other hand, the rates of interest were rising, the lender would endeavor to get in communication with the borrower and have the rate on the loan raised for that day. It is said that certain of the money brokers made good returns on their money invested in call loans by making it very difficult for the borrowers to get in touch with them if there was a drop in the rates, and so have a higher rate rule in the case of their loans than was the current rate in the market. Perhaps their telephone line would be busy and they would be occupied so constantly at such times that the borrowers were not able to get in touch with them.

The preceding description shows the way in which the two rates for loans were at this time determined at the money post. The next event to take place between these two brokers upon the floor who were making a loan was, after the rate and amount had been agreed upon, to exchange a memorandum of the loan stating the amount and the rate of interest, and to send these memoranda to their respective firms. The conditions of the loan thus made were binding upon both the borrowing house, or person, for whom the loan was obtained, and the lending institution for which the lending broker had made the loan. It then remained for the borrower to send the collateral with the necessary margin to the lending institution and for this lender to give the borrower a check for the amount of the loan, provided the collateral proved satisfactory.

The Certified Check.—One of the greatest faults of this method of making loans on the money market was the use of the certified check. The circumstances which brought about the necessity for the certified check were these: The borrower had a loan which had been called by the lender and he thus found it necessary to make a new loan, or liquidate, but he could not make this new loan until he obtained the collateral to give for it, this collateral being held by the bank which had called the loan; on the other hand he was not able to obtain the collateral from the bank which had called his loan until he had given a check for the amount of his loan. This put him in the position of not being able to secure a loan until he obtained his collateral, and of not being able to obtain his collateral until he secured a loan to pay off the one which had been called. The only way out was for the borrower to get a certified check from some third bank where he had a deposit. This check was secured only by the broker's single name paper. That is, it was a promissory note unsecured by any collateral, or by the name of any person other than the borrower. It is true that it was only necessary for him to get this extension of credit for a few hours, but at the same time it caused a huge amount of certification of checks by the banks when any considerable number of loans were called. Loans made upon these certified checks were known as day-loans, being made for a short time during the business day. It should be observed that the day loan proved to be a very safe type of loan, otherwise banks would not have been willing to make them. The banks knew pretty well the people to whom they made these loans, and most of them were made to customers of the banks. While it would seem a rather risky way to do business, losses through day loans were very rare. The main objection to these loans is not any lack of safety to any extent, but rather the very large number of these loans which were made by banks and the consequent large amount of bank credit which was tied up in this way. The main difficulty would arise when there were big withdrawals of funds by the out-of-town banks, which would result in the calling of many of the loans and then there would be attempts of these borrowers to get their loans placed in some of the other banks or agencies in New York.

The major points to be noted in the operation of the money market during this period are the bidding which took place at the money post, the formation of the renewal rate, and the lack of any means of clearing loans when they were to be paid off by the borrower, or called in by the lender.

Second Period—1917-1919—The Money Committee

From September 1917 to January 1919, the New York Call money market was under the supervision and control of the Money Committee, which was itself a sub-committee of the Liberty Loan Committee formed shortly after the United States entered the war. The Money Committee was definitely organized as a sub-committee in September 1917, with Benjamin Strong, Governor of the New York Federal Reserve Bank, as chairman and the following men as members: James S. Alexander, George F. Baker, Walter E. Frew, Bates W. McCenah, Charles H. Sabin, Frank A. Vanderlip, James N. Wallace and Albert H. Wiggin. The reason for the formation of this committee was that when the Liberty Loan Committee was organized in April 1917, one of the first developments which was encountered was the tendency on the part of lenders—both New York City banks and out-of-town banks—to withdraw their loans from the Stock Exchange in order to invest in the new issues of securities being made by the Government. A further reason why the banks wished to withdraw their funds from the Stock Exchange was that they felt that they would have to increase greatly their borrowings from the Federal reserve banks, and so they wished to change these loans for other kinds of investments which would be available for rediscount at the federal reserve banks.

Control of Supply.—Consequently, the Money Committee found it necessary to make up a fund every day which would take care of any deficiencies such as were bound to occur in the Stock Exchange loan account as a result of the calling of loans by banks who desired their funds for other investments. Especially the out-of-town banks found that it was more desirable for them to get their money home again. This fund which the Money Committee made up, at first among the banks which the members represented, was a necessary instrument to keep the rates on call money from rising sharply. If there had been no funds to take the place of those which were withdrawn by the banks, the result would have been that borrowers would have been forced to bid abnormally high rates in order to obtain money and thus the Government would have been seriously hindered in floating its loans because of the extraordinarily high rates which would have been offered for the use of money in the New York money market. Especially as the policy was followed of financing the war cheaply, it would have been impossible to have floated huge loans at low rates of interest if there had been any outside competition with other investments for banks which bore much higher rates of interest and which were safe investments. A still graver result might also have ensued. If, in spite of the high rates which were bid, the banks still continued to withdraw their money, thus leaving an acute demand for money which was not filled at the Exchange, a panic might have followed at the very time when it was absolutely necessary, in order to finance the war, that financial institutions should be on a sound and firm basis, and that the confidence of the people in them should not be shaken. In order that the absolute needs of the money market might be filled, the members of the Committee pledged a pool of money, for Stock Exchange loans, which at first amounted to one hundred millions of dollars. Shortly afterward a contingent fund of another one hundred millions was also pledged for the same purpose.

It was soon found that this fund, as it was organized, bore unevenly on certain banks which did not wish to make these loans but did so because of their interest in the efficient operation of the machinery of the Treasury. On account of this fact a new policy was adopted by the Money Committee in respect to the allotment of this fund among the different banks. Data were gathered as to what banks were in the habit of loaning money on the Exchange and to what amount their loans generally tended. It was found that the banks in the upper part of the city rarely loaned money on the Exchange on account of the character of their business and that the money was mostly supplied by the downtown banks. It was found that the loan account of the Stock Exchange was running between four hundred millions and four hundred and fifty millions at this time, and the Committee attempted, on the basis of the results which they had obtained from their data, to make a fair apportionment of these loans among the different banks. Thus the fund gradually developed from a pool of one hundred millions of dollars, divided among a small number of the larger banks to an apportioning of the whole Stock Exchange loan account, amounting to over four hundred millions of dollars, among all the banks in New York City that were in the habit of making loans upon the Stock Exchange. The banks were virtually compelled to furnish their allotment of money for loans, and if they failed to do so, which was seldom the case, the Money Committee put pressure upon them and forced them to contribute their share. The total number of lenders was about sixty-five.

Control of Demand.—In the discussion so far, the manner in which the Money Committee handled the supply side of the New York money market has been considered. It was, further, necessary for the Committee to keep a firm hand upon the demand side of the money market so that the demands would not be allowed to outrun the supply of the funds which they had thus furnished. This demand side was taken care of by getting daily reports of the members of the Stock Exchange, and by not permitting them to increase their borrowings beyond the amount which they reached upon a certain day. The day selected was the same as that on which the supply of funds necessary for the market had been determined, and so they were able to keep the market stabilized by regulating the demand so that it could not increase beyond the amount of funds which they had undertaken to supply. If the borrowers had increased the amounts of their loans, it would have had the same result as if the banks had decreased the amount available for loans and the same results of inadequate funds to meet the demands would have ensued.

Policies Followed by Money Committee.—At different times during their control, the Money Committee found it necessary to follow two different policies in regard to their control over the money market. The first policy was pursued from the time of the organization until August 1918. During this period the purpose of the Committee was to insure a sufficient fund to take care of the stock exchange transactions. Its policy was one of provision for the imperative needs of the borrowers. At this time the demand seemed to be more intense than the supply, and there was a shortage of funds for the market. Banks at this time did not wish to make loans upon the Exchange and it was the purpose of the Committee to force them to make these loans.

This was the feeling of the banks toward stock exchange loans up to the date of August 1918. About this time the attitude regarding the money market was changing. Borrowers were becoming anxious to enlarge the amount of their loans, while banks did not feel the same necessity of withholding their funds from the market. The Committee found that the tone of the market was becoming highly speculative, and this forced them to change their policy from that of providing for loans, to a policy of restraint and restriction upon the amount of loans made to the members of the Exchange. To put this new plan into operation the daily reports of members of the Exchange were used and estimates of amount of their borrowings made. These reports were strictly confidential and were given only with the understanding that they were in no way to be made public.

In addition to the restriction upon the members which has already been stated, namely that they were not to increase the amounts of their loans above that which was shown at the time chosen by the Committee as the legitimate amount for these loans, another measure to control the speculative tendency was introduced by the Committee. This measure was the increase in the margins of collateral which should be kept against all call loans. The margin required upon mixed collateral, composed of rail and industrial stocks, had previously been twenty per cent, and the margin required on unmixed industrial stocks as collateral had been twenty-five per cent. The Money Committee increased both of these margins and required borrowers making loans to furnish thirty per cent margin upon all loans of the former class, and to furnish thirty-seven and one-half per cent margin upon all loans of the latter class.

A third step which the Committee took in order to keep matters well in hand was to encourage banks to run their time loans for shorter periods than had been customary. Thus they advised banks to make loans for four months instead of six, and for two months instead of three. The reason for this measure was that they did not think it was advisable at that time for the banks to tie up their money for any longer period of time than was absolutely necessary.

To illustrate clearly the policy followed by the Money Committee, the following letter, written in September 1918 by Benjamin Strong, chairman of the Liberty Loan Subcommittee on Money to H. G. S. Noble, President of the New York Stock Exchange may be cited:

My Dear Sir, As you are aware, a subcommittee of the Liberty Loan Committee of this district was appointed on September 5, 1917, and has undertaken certain duties in connection with the New York money market, for securing the most complete cooperation with the Government in its financial program, by all the financial interests of the city.— The work of the subcommittee has met with the cordial cooperation of the important interests connected with the New York money market and there has been maintained an orderly course of affairs in which the supply of funds has been ample for the essential needs. We believe this condition can be continued. It is obvious, however, that for the present there should be devoted to the security market no additional credit beyond the funds now used. Any tendency to expand the collateral loan account should, for the general good, under the present conditions, be checked.

In order that this important situation may be handled in a way that will result in the least possible inconvenience, it is desirable that we should have a complete daily view of stock exchange loans. We recognize the disposition of the Stock Exchange to cooperate in every way toward contributing to the orderly conduct of the money market, and depending upon the patriotic disposition, we now ask the governors of the Stock Exchange to collect, for the confidential use of this committee, daily statements from each member of the Exchange showing in such detail as may be agreed upon in conference, the amount of time and call loans of each Stock Exchange house.

This information will be for the confidential use of the Committee, in whose hands has been placed the responsibility of maintaining an orderly money market. The reports will be asked during a temporary period. At present it is impossible for us to say for just how long a period they will be needed. We will be obliged if you will ask the members of the Exchange to begin these reports at the earliest date practicable.

Lest any possible misunderstanding arise as to the object of this request, I am directed by the committee to explain that this is only one of a number of measures being undertaken by the committee with the object of exercising, by mutual understanding among the institutions and firms of this city, such reasonable and necessary control of the employment of credit as will insure no interference with the financial operations of the Government in conducting the war.

Accurate information as to the amount of bank credit being employed for Stock Exchange purposes will be useful in attaining these objects.

I am directed by the committee to express its cordial appreciation of the spirit of cooperation which has been shown by the officers and members of the Stock Exchange in matters of this kind, which feeling is shared by the officers of the Federal Reserve Bank.

The control of the Money Committee lasted until January 10, 1919. At this time there was a countrywide cry to get back to "business as usual" and a relinquishment of all war measures. The officers of the Stock Exchange felt that they were fully able to deal with the situation and requested that the numerous measures which were inaugurated during the foregoing period should be abandoned. On the other hand, the members of the Money Committee were perfectly willing to withdraw from the field and had continued during the latter part of their term only at the special request of the Treasury. As a consequence of the feeling that business should now get back to normal, and that the conditions no longer warranted such harsh measures, the Money Committee relinquished their control January 10, 1919. At this time the committee published three general conclusions which they had reached:

1. "That the control of the Stock Exchange Committee may for the present be suspended."
2. "That the Stock Exchange authorities be requested to continue to receive from the members of the Exchange daily reports of their borrowings until after the next Liberty Loan is placed."
3. "That the definite arrangement made with a large group of New York banks for furnishing funds for Stock Exchange loans, if and as required, should now be terminated."

During this period in the history of the money market the "money post" was done away with, and the money desk was substituted for it. The functions of this money desk will be fully dealt with when the third period in the history of the money market is discussed. The reasons for its inauguration as a substitute for the money post should, however, be given here. When the Money Committee took control of the loan account of the money market, they naturally found it necessary to get figures concerning demand and supply. They wished to know whether or not the banks were all furnishing the funds allotted to them and also it was necessary to be sure what brokers were borrowing money and to see that no broker was able to obtain more than his share of loans. The money post did not offer the facilities necessary for such registration of lenders and borrowers, consequently, the money desk with its clerk was substituted to serve this purpose. After the dissolution of the Money Committee, it was found that this desk had proved so satisfactory that it was decided to keep it in operation and to abandon entirely the old money post.

As the Money Committee had complete control over the demand and supply of money, it is obvious that they were also able to exercise complete control over the rates at which this money was loaned. There was no reason at all for a borrower to bid high rates for call money, because he was not allowed to make loans exceeding the amount established by the Committee as a limit, and he was always assured that he would be able to get funds to the amount which the Committee had fixed as his limit. Thus all elements of competition for the use of money were eliminated, because this was a period in which money was rationed just as any other commodity might be during war-time.

In conclusion it should be noted that there was not yet any clearing house for loans, so that during this period loans were terminated and made between the borrowing houses and lending institutions in the same way as during the first period which has already been discussed. The rates at which money was loaned were not decided freely by the lender and borrower, but were virtually fixed by the Money Committee through its control over demand and supply.

Third Period—Present Methods

The third period in the history of the New York Money Market begins in January 1919. There are many points of difference in the organization of the Money Market as it exists now and as it existed before the War. The most obvious point of difference is the use of the money desk on the floor of the Exchange. The money clerk in charge may be said to register the demand for and the supply of money. Banks, after the business day opens, estimate the money available for the money market and then call up the broker who represents them upon the floor of the Exchange and state to him what money they wish to loan upon the market and at what rate they are willing to loan it. If their daily balance is larger than usual they may have some fresh funds to loan. If, on the other hand, their statement shows that they have a debit with the Clearing House, or that they have other large obligations to meet, they may call in some of the call loans which they have outstanding. If there are any loans to be called it is done by the bank itself and not by its broker on the floor of the Exchange.

Then if the broker has received money, or rather orders to loan money, he goes over to the money desk and tells the clerk there what funds he has and at what rate they are to be loaned. The rate is either a fixed rate, for example, five per cent, or the bank, as is generally the case, may give the broker orders to loan its money at the market rate, whatever that rate may be. By this method all the money available for the call money market on the Exchange is registered at the money desk. The clerk sets down in his entry book the various amounts of money, the rates at which these amounts will be loaned, and also the names of the brokers who are intrusted with loaning these various amounts.

Making a Loan on the Floor of the Exchange.— After the market opens, the broker who wishes to borrow goes to the money desk and asks the clerk what money is available, who is handling it and at what rate it is to be loaned. If the conditions do not satisfy him—if, for example, the rate seems too high —he may leave an order with the clerk that he desires to borrow a certain amount of money at a certain rate of interest. If, on the other hand, he thinks the money already offered is satisfactory, he will obtain from the clerk the name of the broker who has the money to lend, or several names if he so desires, and he will hunt out these brokers on the floor of the

Exchange. After this part of the transaction of the loan has been completed the clerk has done his part in the making of the loan, and he does not again enter into the business. He merely gives the information necessary for the borrower and lender to get in touch with each other. The next step in the making of the loan concerns only the borrowing and lending brokers. When the borrower finds the lender he wishes, he states how much money he desires to obtain and what rate he is willing to pay. If the rates are satisfactory to both parties, they agree to make the loan, or there may take place a small compromise as to the rate as a result of a difference of opinion as to just what the rate should be. When the first loan is made in the morning the market rate is established. This loan is reported to the money desk by the broker who has left his name with the clerk and has since either made a loan to someone or secured a loan. The clerk then posts the rate of the loan on the wall back of the desk under a sign which reads "market rate." Of course, when a new loan is made at a subsequent and different rate, the clerk takes down the old market rate and posts the new rate at which the last loan was made.

After this much of the transaction has been completed by the borrowing and lending brokers upon the floor of the Exchange, they both have accomplished all they have to do in making the loan. At this time the lending broker reports to the lending institution to whom its funds have been loaned and the rate at which they have been loaned, while the borrowing broker sends a similar report of the loan to his office. These reports are only memoranda and are unsigned. This terminates that part of the transaction which takes place upon the floor of the Exchange. What remains is for the borrowing house to deliver the security collateral to the lending institution and to obtain the funds from the lender, but the brokers upon the floor have nothing to do with that part of the transaction.

Thus far in the discussion the main point of difference between the present system and the system used before the War is the way in which the borrower and lender get in touch with one another and the manner in which each is able to judge the general trend of the market. The method is far superior to that of the old money post, and saves a great amount of time and trouble for all the parties concerned. Neither the borrower nor the lender is compelled to stay at a certain post on the floor and bid or offer money. The loans are quietly made after the conditions have been observed and much of the former confusion and excitement which was characteristic of the "money crowd" is in this way avoided.

Determination of the Renewal Rate.—Briefly stated, the renewal rate may be said to be today that rate at which the largest borrowers and lenders of money on call agree to renew their loans for the day. Our present purpose is to examine exactly how this rate is agreed upon. Shortly after the business day opens and after the banks have got their clearing house statements, so that they know approximately how they stand for the day, the Stock Clearing Corporation, the functions and organization of which will be explained later, calls up the largest lending institutions, which will number about fifteen, and asks them what they think the proper renewal rate should be upon call loans for the day, and how much money is available. When the different opinions of the largest lenders have been ascertained as to what the renewal rate should be and how much money is available for the money market, the next step is to question the brokers upon the floor of the Exchange, who are going to be the largest borrowers, and find out how much money they will want to borrow for the day and what rate of interest they think should be paid. From these two sources, the Stock Clearing Corporation is able to get a very accurate report as to what the supply of money will be for the day, and also what the needs will be upon the demand side of the money market. At the same time the Stock Clearing Corporation takes into consideration what the conditions were in the previous day of business and how much money was offered which was not taken, and at what rate. There will always, except in times of panic, be some money offered which is not taken on account of the fact that a few allotments of money will be sent to the market to be placed at a rate which the borrower considers too high and which will be under-bid by all other lending institutions. Each loan made through the day is reported to the Stock Clearing Corporation and the rate at which the loan is made. All changes in the rate are also reported as they occur. At different times during the day they get reports from the floor as to what money is offered, at what rate it is offered, and how much money has been taken. Thus they have their hand continually upon the pulse of the money market. Moreover, they get the reports of all sales in the stocks upon the Exchange, and these sales amount to about 92 per cent of all sales taking place in New York. This gives them an opportunity to keep accurate figures as to the general trend of market prices, which is a very good way of determining how much money the market is likely to absorb in the immediate future. Of course as the number of sales of stock increases, the demand for money is likely to increase, especially if there is a strong bull movement in certain stocks. Then there is bound to be more buying on margin and the consequent need for more call loans to enable the participators in this movement to carry these stocks. Unfortunately the Stock Clearing Corporation cannot have such complete figures on the total amounts of money that are loaned on call, because not all of the call loans are made on the Stock Exchange—but many of them are made in either of the two outside markets which have been described. Estimates as to the percentage of call loans that are made on the floor of the Exchange range from about 60 to 80 per cent of all those made in New York City.

The Stock Clearing Corporation keeps a most interesting and instructive chart which shows the average rate at which money is loaned upon the Exchange each day and also indicates the renewal rate on call loans for the day. From this chart the Stock Clearing Corporation is able to tell how nearly the renewal rate coincides with the average rate upon all call loans made upon the floor. They can thus see at a glance what the general trend of the price for money is, and may adjust their renewal rate with it. Thus, if the renewal rate runs slightly above the average rate for all loans made during the day, all other factors remaining equal, the renewal rate will be dropped slightly the next day, so as to coincide as closely as possible with this average rate.

Factors which Determine the Call Loan Rate.— Following is a list of some of the most important factors which affect the call money market. They will be shown to have influence upon the rate of interest which is charged for call loans.

1. Local Condition of the Money Market
   (a) Average rate of call money during the day.
   (b) Renewal rate on call loans.
   (c) Discount call money market.
2. Factors relating to Federal Reserve activities
   (a) Federal reserve shiftings.
   (b) Federal reserve bills bought in the open market.
   (c) Federal reserve discount rate.

(d) Federal reserve volume discount.
(e) Crop moving.

3. International Finance Conditions
   (a) Foreign exchange rates.
   (b) Foreign situation.
   (c) Gold importation and exportation.
   (d) Bank of England rate.
4. Permanent Investments
   (a) Course of the bond market.
   (b) Course of stock market—strength or weakness—volume of sales.
   (c) Reorganization payments.
   (d) Syndicate payment. (Dates ahead.)
5. Financing by Governmental Bodies
   (a) Government financing. (Dates ahead.)
   (b) City and state bond issues.
6. Time Money
7. Condition of Banks
   (a) Clearing House Bank Statement.
   (b) Reserve in the member banks, and Federal Reserve Bank Statement.
8. Acceptance Market
9. Prices of Commodities

These different factors will be considered in their order. First we will take up the first group given above and see what effect they have on the rates of call loans.

1. Local Conditions of the Money Market.—All three of the factors given in this first group are closely inter-related. The average rate of call money during the day has an effect on the renewal rate, because, as has been shown, there is an attempt to keep the two rates as close together as possible by checking up any difference which might arise between them. The renewal rate is generally taken by the public, that is, by those who know anything about the money market, as a very good indication of what the condition of the call money market is. Many of those brokers who lend money on call are accustomed to loaning it at the renewal rate, because this rate is taken as one which is carefully calculated by those who are best qualified to do so. So much confidence now exists in the fixing of the renewal rate that it is generally taken for granted that it will follow the average rate for call loans very closely, and statistics have shown that the two rates do not differ considerably. The discount call money market bears somewhat the same relation to the call money rate as the discount rates of federal reserve banks bear to the interest rates which are charged by banks for funds. The discount call money market is taken as a very good indication of the general condition of the call money market, because it shows what the larger dealers in these loans think is a justifiable rate of interest.

2. Factors Relating to Federal Reserve Activities.—The second group of factors have to do chiefly with those activities of the Federal Reserve System which have noticeable results in the call money market. First take Federal reserve shiftings; if there is a shift of funds from the New York Federal Reserve Bank to some other federal reserve bank, either voluntarily or by the order of the Federal Reserve Board, the result will be that there will be a smaller amount of credit facilities to be furnished to the members of the system in the New York district. When money is fairly easy, such a change would not make much difference in the call money market. But when money is tight, if some of the funds were withdrawn from the New York district, the result would be that banks would have less money available for the call money market. The national banks always keep on the look-out to see what the condition of the federal reserve bank of their district is so that they may be able to tell how far to go in regard to the extension of credit, whether it be on the call money market, or to their own customers. Furthermore, if there is a voluntary shifting of federal reserve funds, for the reason that there is more profit in their employment in other districts, there may be a rise in the call money rates in an attempt to get funds back to New York. This, however, is only likely to take place when there is a shortage of money in New York or when a speculative movement is under way.

Federal reserve bills bought in the open market may readily be seen to affect the call money rate because of the fact that the banks will tend to invest their temporary funds in that which is the most profitable to them. If the rate of profit is higher in buying federal reserve bills than in investing on the call money market, the banks will invest their money in the former way. As a result the call loan rate will have to be high enough to compete with the federal reserve bills.

The federal reserve discount rate serves to show the banks at what rate they will be able to borrow funds from the federal reserve bank of their district. It gives an indication of what the policy of the federal reserve bank will be in the extension of credit. When the banks are in a strong position, that is, when they have plenty of funds, they may not be at all dependent on the federal reserve bank for the extension of credit, and in this case they may go their own way in regard to the amount of money that they lend and the rate of interest which they charge. At the same time banks generally take warning of a rise in the discount rate of the federal reserve bank, and they know that that is a warning to go rather slowly in the further inflation of credit. The result is that there is a general rise in the interest rates when there is a rise in the discount rate, and call money rates rise with the rest.

In the same way the volume of federal reserve discount is related to the call money market. As there is an increase in the volume of credit which is extended by the federal reserve banks without any addition to the gold holdings, the amount of credit which is available is decreased, since there is a reduction in the reserves of the federal reserve bank according to the increase in the volume of discount.

In this same group may be considered also the

effect of crop moving on the call money rate. Briefly it may be said that when there is more need and effective demand for funds in other parts of the country, there will be an exodus of funds from New York City. So when there is a large call for funds in other parts of the country for the moving of the crops, there are withdrawals of funds from the New York money market. This need for funds in other parts of the country decreases the amount which is kept by out-of-town banks in call loans, as they withdraw it to use in their local districts. More will be said later about this particular phase of the subject.

3. **International Finance Conditions.**—In the third group are those factors which have an effect on the world-wide financial conditions and also reflect these conditions in the New York money market. They all indicate the amount of credit that will be available in New York City. Take gold importation and exportation: As the amount of the gold in the country increases, other factors remaining equal, the amount of credit available will be increased, since all bank credit is based on the supply of gold in the country. As gold collects in the federal reserve banks they have a greater lending power, and the interest rates over the country at large are apt to be lower than when there is a scarcity of gold with the consequent reduction of the possible expansion in the total volume of funds which can be loaned. When there is a large exportation of gold, the money rates, and

the call money rate are apt to go up. Foreign exchange rates and the foreign situation serve to indicate the flow of credit, whether it be to this country, or away from the United States to other countries. If the exchange rates are against us, and it becomes cheaper to ship gold, there will probably be a smaller volume of credit available in this country. If the exchange rates are in our favor, and there are likely to be shipments of gold to this country, there is likely to be a drop of interest rates.

In regard to the foreign situation, it may be said that if there is any large amount of lending of funds to the foreign countries there will, for the time, be less money to be loaned in this country. With the increase in the amount of the foreign investments there is likely to be a decrease in the volume of money which is loaned on the money market, because of the fact that some of the funds will only be loaned on the Stock Exchange until some permanent investment is found for them. The Bank of England rate is a good indication of the way in which the world's funds are flowing. England has been the financial center of the world and she has been able to control the outward flow of gold to foreign countries largely by raising the Bank of England rate. When there is an increase in this rate, we may assume that there will be a temporary cessation of the flow of gold out of England, or maybe a flow of gold from this country to England. As a result, the raising of the rate will have a tendency to create a comparatively tighter money market in this country and a consequent increase in the call money rates.

4. **Permanent Investments.**—The fourth group of factors have to do with the effect of permanent investments upon the call money rates. If one or more new bond issues are being launched, there will be some withdrawals from the New York money market by those investors who have put their money into call loans only until they are able to find some other more permanent investment. Savings banks may invest money in call loans when some bonds reach maturity, and while waiting for some other bonds which they wish to buy to be put on the market.

The course of the stock market is of great importance because of the demand that is created for call loans under different conditions of this market. If there is a rise in the prices of some of the more speculative stocks, and an increase in the volume of sales, if—in other words, there is a strong bull movement—there will be a larger demand for call loans. More people will be buying stocks on margin with the hopes of holding them for a while and selling them for a profit, and in these purchases on margin it has been shown that a large use is made of call loans. When the market is on one of these upward swings, it is always likely that the money rates will go up, and it is in such times that the high call money rates have existed in the past. This statement does not refer to panic conditions, which are exceptional.

While, of course, the highest call money rates have existed in the time of panics, these rates lasted only for a little while. On the other hand, a bullish movement may last for several months and during this extended period the money rates will rule high. When, however, the stock market has been weak, and there has been a small volume of sales, there is generally plenty of money which may be obtained in call loans; the supply runs far in excess of the demand, and the result is that the call money rate may at such times drop to below one per cent. A point may be noted here in respect to syndicate issues. Such issues are financed by means of call loans, and the result of this method of financing is that at a time when large amounts of these syndicate issues are being put out there will be a bigger demand for call loans. The result of this demand is that the rate will be higher than would otherwise be the case.

The effect of syndicate payments is to lessen the amount of money available for the call money market, for as has been said before, much of the money which is loaned on the market comes from corporations when they are collecting funds for such payments. In the same way reorganization payments lessen the funds which will be offered on the market and so tend to advance the rate of interest which will be paid on call loans.

5. **Financing by Government Bodies.**—In the fifth group the effect of financing by the federal govern-

ment, and of city and state bond issues is considered. Of course the increases which may take place in the funds which are used for the purchase of these bonds will be accompanied with a decrease, usually, in the amount of money which is offered on the money market. Many of these securities are bought by those corporations which lend their idle funds in call loans. When there is a new offering of these securities there is a strong chance that some of the money will be withdrawn from the call money market in order to purchase these permanent investments.

6. Time Money.—The next factor in the table given is time money. The rates of interest on time loans vary not only with the conditions of the money market at the time when the loan is negotiated, but also with what may be expected as to money conditions in the near future during the life of the time loan. Thus, if the lender considers that money will be tighter a month from now than it is at present, if he is making a time loan which is to run for three months, he will take this fact into consideration and charge a higher rate of interest on the loan than would seem to be warranted by the present conditions of the money market. Call loan rates must, to a certain extent, compete with these time money rates, and the result will be that the call money rates will be apt to go up as there is an advance in the time money rates. A discounting of the future takes place in the time money market.

7. **Condition of the Banks.**—Two more factors are here considered: the clearing house bank statement and reserve in the member banks in conjunction with the Federal Reserve Bank Statement. Formerly the clearing house statement of the New York banks was of far greater significance than is the case at present. Before the enactment of the Federal Reserve Act, the amount of loanable funds could be figured fairly closely by inspection of this statement, which used to come out Friday afternoon. Those who were interested in the money market were able to determine closely the amount of loans, investments, and discounts; the amount of deposits, both demand and time; reserve with legal depositories; cash in the vaults of the banks; and the amount of surplus reserves which the banks held. As a result it was possible to figure the amount of surplus funds available for the extension of credit, and from this to estimate roughly what would be the condition of the money market. It was found that the statement was so likely to upset the loan market that the statement is now put out on Saturday so that the loan market will not be thrown into confusion at the end of the week; by the time Saturday comes all the call loans run until the next Monday at the rate at which they were made or renewed on Friday.

Since the establishment of the Federal Reserve System, however, the amount of surplus reserve of banks cannot be taken as an accurate index of the ability of the banks to extend loans. Banks are now able to extend their loans by borrowing from the federal reserve bank. They send in collateral which will be discounted by the federal reserve bank and thus increase their reserves far in excess of the amount which they would otherwise have. The reserve is not now measured by cash, but by the character of the assets available for receiving credits at the federal reserve bank, and by the ability and willingness of the federal reserve bank to extend such credits. As a result of this change the statement of the New York Clearing House has lost much of its former significance. The two things which are of importance in connection with the ability of the member banks to get credit from the federal reserve bank are: the reserve ratio of the federal reserve bank, which indicates the amount of credit which the federal reserve bank may extend, and the discount rate, which indicates the willingness of the federal reserve bank to extend such credit. The federal reserve bank must keep a minimum of 35 per cent gold in its vaults against the deposits of the member banks which the members must make in order to obtain credit. When this reserve approaches the minimum which is required by law, we should expect the interest rates to go up as a result of the fact that the federal reserve bank would raise its discount rate in order to discourage any further increase in the amount of credit which the member banks would seek.

If the Federal Reserve System followed the policy of allowing all banks to obtain about all the credit which the federal reserve banks could extend to them, there might be no great increase in the interest rates until the time was almost reached when the federal reserve banks would be unable to make any further extensions of credit. As an actual fact, the federal reserve bank usually stops, or discourages, the banks long before their gold reserves approach the minimum. They attempt to stabilize the credit situation so that the banks may serve the best needs of the country and so that there may be no unnecessary inflation of credit which might lead to disastrous results for the prosperity of the country. The discount rates are not raised when the federal reserve bank finds any further large extensions of credit to the member banks to be impossible, but rather when they are thought to be unwise. As a consequence of this policy of the federal reserve banks, there is an indirect control of these banks over the money market. When there is a rise in the discount rates, this is most likely to be accompanied by an increase in the call money rate, for it is an indication that in the opinion of the federal reserve banks there should be no further large expansion of credit.

Whether these increases in the discount rate will be effective in increasing the rates for money, or how far they will be effective, may depend somewhat on the conditions of the member banks. If they have a large amount of funds which they wish to loan, and are not in need of borrowing from the federal reserve bank, then they may not take the warning of the federal reserve bank as to further extension of credit by it to them, and may make loans at a rate of interest as low as that prevailing before there was any increase in the discount rate. This will all depend upon the policy of the individual banks, but it seems that the banks in general are taking heed to the danger signals which are given by the federal reserve banks of different districts in the form of increased discount rates. In times when the condition of the member banks does not allow them to increase the amount of their loans without recourse to the federal reserve bank, the rates of the federal reserve bank must be effective in curtailing the amount of funds loaned by the member banks. They will certainly not loan money at a lower rate of interest than that which they must pay the federal reserve bank, and thus as the discount rate of the federal reserve bank goes up, and the member bank has to pay more for the funds which it obtains from it to loan to individuals, the result is that the member bank must charge the individual more for his loan. In this connection loans in general have been spoken of, but of course as the interest rates on loans in general increased, there would be an increase in the call money rate, probably to a greater extent than in any of the other forms of loans, since there would be less surplus money to be loaned on the money market. As banks find that there is a shortage of credit for their own customers they are likely to be compelled to withdraw funds from the call money market in order to meet the demands of their customers, even if it were more profitable to leave the money invested in the call loans.

8. The Acceptance Market.—The acceptance market competes with the call loan market in somewhat the same way as does the time money market. The result is that an increase in the return which lenders will get on money which is loaned on acceptances will cause an increase in the call money rate. The bank lending its money in the form of acceptances always has the advantage of being able to discount these acceptances with the federal reserve bank. If it finds that it wishes to get additional funds from the federal reserve bank, it may discount such paper which is eligible. As collateral loans, based on stock exchange securities, are not eligible for rediscount, the bank holding acceptances has an advantage in that it may depend on the federal reserve bank for funds. In periods when money is tight banks will give the rediscount privilege more consideration, as they may wish to get assistance from the federal reserve bank, and this fact will cause them to favor the acceptance market rather than the call money market. This is especially true of the out-of-town banks because they are not closely associated with the money market and thus have little interest in it outside of a convenient place to loan their funds in a very liquid form. The Federal Reserve System has fostered the growth of the acceptance market and has encouraged the country banks to loan their funds in acceptances rather than be dependent on the New York money market.

9. **Prices of Commodities.**—The last factor in the list is the prices of commodities. These have an effect on the call loan market because of the effect which they have on business and speculation. When there is an increase in the prices of commodities, there will be a strong stimulus for an increase in business and in production. This will be accompanied usually with an increase in the prices of securities and probably a bull movement on the stock market. Then there will be more purchases of securities on margin, with the result that there will be a larger demand for call loans with an increase in the rate of interest on these loans. At the same time there will be larger demands for all other forms of credit in the field of time loans and this will still further shorten the supply of funds for the call loan market in proportion to the demand for such loans. At these periods of rising prices we generally enter into the upward swing of the business cycle and during these periods the interest rates rise; this results from the fact that there is a greater demand for funds in almost all fields, with no corresponding increase in the supply.

On the other hand, when there is a drop in the commodity prices there is likely to be less demand for funds. Production and business in general will slacken and these same men who wished to increase the amount of their borrowings in the time of business activity and rising prices will now have less need for such large amounts of credit. With the reduction of the demand for credit there will be large amounts of funds seeking investment; the result will be that the money market will be flooded with idle funds that will be loaned at almost any price. This is shown to be true in the period of rising prices after the war, when the call money rates were extremely high. At times call loans yielded the lender as high as ten per cent, and on a few occasions even higher. Then in the depression and dull business period which came after 1920, the call money rates began to descend. In 1924, when business was very dull, and the reserves of the banks were piling up with no immediate use for them, call money could barely be loaned at two per cent.

The Renewal Rate and the Rates Paid by Individuals.—To go back now to the Stock Clearing Corporation, they attempt to fix the renewal rate with due consideration to all these factors discussed, which are shown to affect the supply of funds available for the call money market, and hence the interest rate for call loans. The rate is fixed by the Stock Clearing Corporation in conjunction with some of the members of the governing committee of the Stock Exchange. This rate is so accurately and justly fixed that it is followed by nearly all borrowers and lenders of money upon the Stock Exchange money market. The reason for the general acceptance of this rate is that both lenders and borrowers think that it is fairly and skillfully fixed. The skill is owing to the information which the Stock Clearing Corporation has concerning the money market.

It should be borne in mind that this renewal rate is not binding upon all borrowers or lenders. If any borrower considers that the rate is too high he may call his loan and attempt to make it outside the Stock Exchange at a lower rate. The same thing is true of the lender who thinks that he is not receiving enough for his money; he may call in his loans and try to make them at a figure higher than the market rate, or he may withdraw them from the money market altogether and invest them in something else. This often happens in the case of out-of-town banks who only lend money upon the money market when they find high rates of interest to attract their funds, or when they have little use for the employment of their money at home. One might be led to say that the money could not be obtained outside at a lower rate, because the supply was controlled by the persons who determine the rate of interest at which the call loans are to be renewed. Such is not the case, and there is no control of the rates on call loans which are made outside of the Stock Exchange nor any control of the supply. If the borrower finds that he must pay as much outside of the Stock Exchange as he would have to pay for his loan made on the floor, it is not a proof that there is control of the call money market, but rather that the rate on the Exchange is a fair rate.

The call loan does not, strictly speaking, last for just twenty-four hours, and if the borrower does not pay off his loan within exactly this limit of time he is not compelled to pay interest for another day. If, for example, a broker obtains a loan at ten o'clock in the morning, when the market first opens, he may wait the next morning until the renewal rate is posted before he decides whether he wishes to keep the loan made on the Stock Exchange, or whether he prefers to pay off this loan and attempt to make the loan outside the Stock Exchange at a lower rate. As a consequence, brokers have the advantage of being able to look over the different money markets in New York before they decide whether they will continue their present loans or will change them. The broker is supposed to pay off his loan in the early afternoon, at the latest, if he does not expect to hold it and pay interest upon it for that day. As a rule, the brokers decide in the morning whether or not they desire to continue their loans, so that the bank will have better opportunity to relend the money again elsewhere. It has been found that the rate is fairly fixed so that banks and borrowers alike almost invariably follow the renewal rate as it is established from day to day, and ordinarily there is very little shifting of loans on account of interest rates. In the termination of loans the advantages seem to be with the borrowing broker in case he wishes to make use of them.

After the renewal rate has been determined—usually about 10:45 in the morning—it is posted upon the wall behind the money desk alongside of the prevailing market rate. The rate then stands for twenty-four hours as the renewal rate for call loans and does not change until the next morning when it is again determined for the next day. This method of determining the renewal rate for call loans is a sharp contrast with the method used before the War. Formerly there was no such organization as now exists to aid in a just determination of what the rate should be, but the rate was determined individually. Different lenders and borrowers had different views as to what the market conditions were; and fixed the renewal rate in accordance with their opinions of the market conditions. It was impossible for any individual lender or borrower to have as complete a knowledge of the conditions affecting demand and supply as is now had by the Stock Clearing Corporation, where all the data concerning demand and supply are collected. The result is that the renewal rate is now more just than the different rates which existed formerly, where they might favor some borrower and be disadvantageous to some other borrowers.

Present Clearance of Loans.—Another change in the loan market is the way in which loans are now cleared. Certain differences from former periods are apparent in the way a loan is handled after it is made on the floor of the Exchange. Earlier in this chapter it has been explained that loans which were shifted from one bank to another required the borrower to secure temporary credit for a few hours with some third bank. This has now been made largely unnecessary by the operation of the Stock Clearing Corporation. This corporation was formed in 1892, but the clearing of loans was not inaugurated until 1921. Instead of the one branch which formerly existed for the clearance of stocks alone, it has now been divided into two branches, the Night Clearing Branch and the Day Clearing Branch. The Night Clearing Branch clears only stocks, whereas the Day Clearing Branch clears not only the stock balances, but also loans based upon security collateral. This clearance of loans has made the certification of a check by a third bank unnecessary while the broker is shifting his loan.

The actual clearing of loans is performed in the offices of the Day Clearing Branch, which are now in the basement of the Stock Exchange Building. A very good description is given by Mr. Meeker in "The Work of the New York Stock Exchange." * He says:

> Its quarters consist of a single large room, fringed upon three sides by rows of cages, each of which is occupied by a representative of one of the large New York banking institutions which loan money on call. The center of the room is occupied by a hollow square formed by ten large cages in which the accounts of the Exchange members who employ the Stock Clearing Corporation are kept. Inside this square are the managerial offices of the Day Clearing Branch. In the corner of the room is a separate cage for the distributing department with a special entrance on Broad Street for the messengers of clearing members

* J. Edward Meeker: The Work of the New York Stock Exchange. 1922.

who come to deliver the tickets employed in the work of the clearance. The two main entrances to the Day Clearing Branch on Broad and New Streets are closely guarded and the whole office is equipped with the most modern and complete protective devices.

Originally the booths around the walls were twenty-nine in number and only twenty-nine lending institutions could participate in the clearance of loans. This lack of space is being overcome by the large extension of the Stock Exchange Building which is nearing completion. The members of the Stock Clearing Corporation are divided into two classes; the one class consists of "clearing members" who usually appear in the market as borrowers and the other class are the "lending members." These lending members pay no charges to the Stock Clearing Corporation and do not own any of its stock. The whole of the stock of the corporation is owned by the New York Stock Exchange. The expenses of the Corporation are entirely paid by a clearance charge upon the money value of stocks cleared.

Making a Call Loan Through the Stock Clearing Corporation.—When the borrower and lender upon the floor of the Exchange have both sent their memoranda to their respective offices situated some place in the city, the following routine is gone through, providing of course, that both the borrowing house and the lending institution are represented in the Day Clearing Branch of the Stock Clearing Corporation. The borrower makes out a form in quadruplicate with the clearing number of his house at its head. This form is called the new loan agreement. This agreement contains a formal statement setting forth that the lender has agreed to loan the borrower a certain amount of money at a certain interest rate. This is followed by an itemized list which gives the names, the prices, and number of shares of the various securities which are put up as security collateral against the loan. The borrower then sends these four forms around to the lender, and the lender at this point examines the list of securities given as collateral and passes judgment as to whether or not they are satisfactory to him. If they are not satisfactory he will call upon the borrower to substitute some other securities which will be acceptable. After this point has been settled, the lender takes two of the loan agreements for his own use and returns two of them, signed by him, to the representative of the borrower.

The borrower then sends these two signed forms to the Stock Clearing Corporation, having them delivered at the particular booth in the center of the room where his account is kept. Thus the borrower notifies the Stock Clearing Corporation that it is to act in making a loan for him. The lender then sends his representative around to the Stock Clearing Corporation with the two forms of the loan agreement which have been given to him by the borrower and with a check for the amount of the loan, which is made out to the Stock Clearing Corporation for the account of the borrower. The lender then secures the collateral for the loan from the Stock Clearing Corporation and has only to see that the securities given him are identical with those which appear upon the loan agreement. These securities will have been deposited by the borrower with the Stock Clearing Corporation, if they have not already been deposited there before by some previous lender with whom this same borrower has settled earlier in the day for the amount of the loan.

The operation ends with the crediting of the check to the account of the borrower. The lender has now secured his collateral and the borrower has secured the amount of his loan. One point worthy of observation is that these new loan agreements are necessarily made through the Stock Clearing Corporation only up to 2:45 p. m., after which time the lender may insist that they be made "ex," which means that they must be done in the old way as before the operation of this Day Clearing Branch. In this case the collateral for the loan is transferred directly from the borrower to the lender and is not held at all by the Stock Clearing Corporation. This results in the old necessary evil of the borrower's obtaining credit from another bank on his promissory note so that he may be able to transfer his securities from the bank calling the loan to the bank making the new loan to him.

Paying Off an Old Loan Through the Stock Clearing Corporation.—Old loans are paid off through the

Stock Clearing Corporation. A call loan, as said before, may be terminated in either of two ways; it may be called by the lender, or the borrower may notify the lender that he wishes to pay off his loan. In either case this notification is given directly between the borrower and lender and it should be recalled that no loans are called after 12:15.

The borrower who is paying off his loan through the Stock Clearing Corporation, of which he must be a member to enjoy this privilege, fills out a quadruplicate form which is much the same as that used in making a new loan. Three of these forms he signs and these three forms are used in paying off the loan. The form contains, as does that for making new loans, the amount of the loan, the interest, and the list of securities with their prices, and the number of shares of each. The borrower also fills out a memorandum making the amount of the loan and interest payable to the lender. This memorandum is of no use as a check until it is signed by the Stock Clearing Corporation.

These three forms are sent to the lender by the borrower and the lender detaches one of them, returning the other two to the borrower's representative, who delivers them, together with the memorandum, to the Day Branch of the Stock Clearing Corporation. The lender then sends the loan envelope containing the securities, which were collateral for the loan, to the Day Clearing Branch, where they are presented at the cage where the borrower's account is kept. The contents of the envelope are compared with the list of securities on the face of the form which has already been delivered by the borrower. If these two lists agree, the clerk keeps the securities and credits them to the account of the borrower. A representative of the Stock Clearing Corporation then fills out the memorandum with his signature and the designation of the bank at which it is to be presented for payment. The bank designated may be any of the banks of the city in which the Stock Clearing Corporation keeps funds deposited for these clearings.

If the borrower wishes to withdraw any of the securities held by the Stock Clearing Corporation, he is allowed to do so providing that the amount withdrawn does not exceed the amount of his credit at that time with the Corporation, and furthermore provided that he either establishes other credits or sends the Corporation a certified check for the amount before two hours have elapsed. In the event that the borrower withdraws more securities than the amount of his credit he must forthwith deposit with the Stock Clearing Corporation a certified check for that amount which his withdrawals exceed his credit. The securities may be withdrawn from the Stock Clearing Corporation by the borrower at the end of the day after his account with the Corporation has been balanced for the day.

Loans are now made and cleared through the Stock Clearing Corporation in the way just described. The great saving in the number of checks drawn, which is made possible by the Night Clearing Branch, is a result of the fact that the members of the Stock Clearing Corporation merely clear balances under the present system, whereas they formerly were forced to secure credit and give checks for every individual sale.

Before the inauguration of the present clearing system, brokers were forced to make a great many deliveries of stocks around the city and also found it necessary to draw separate checks for the majority of the individual sales of securities. Of course there was a certain amount of informal clearing which went on before the present system was put into operation, but it was unorganized and very far from universal. Under the present clearing system, the members do not make individual deliveries of stock sales, as was the case formerly, but settle up their account with the Stock Clearing Corporation at the end of each business day. If they end the day with a debit, they must remit a check to the Corporation for its amount; if they end the day with a favorable balance, they may withdraw the amount of the balance. It is easily understood that such a system as the present one must save an enormous amount of credit and cause a large reduction in the total number of checks drawn. There has been so great an increase in the number of transactions in late years that it would now be impossible for the New York brokers to make separate deliveries around the city for each sale, unless they used a very much larger labor force. It would be far more expensive and inconvenient to operate at present without the aid of the Stock Clearing Corporation. It has been estimated that this new method of clearing loans and stocks saves 92 per cent in the total number of checks drawn and 60 per cent in the number of certified checks drawn.

Conclusion.—In conclusion of this chapter it should be noted that the present system of operation of the call money market on the New York Stock Exchange differs from the system used before the War in three major respects.

1. The money desk as compared with the old money post.
2. The method of determining the renewal rate for call loans.
3. The method of making new loans and clearing old loans through a clearing house for that purpose in contrast with the old method of certification of checks based upon the single name paper of the brokers, as was the practice under the old system.

CHAPTER III

VARIATIONS IN THE DEMAND AND SUPPLY OF FUNDS

No Control Over Supply and Demand.—In any market in which competition is free, the price of the commodity dealt in is determined by the demand and the supply of that commodity. This holds true whether the market happens to be one in which credit is the commodity, or bread, or any other economic good. In the New York money market the price of credit is the interest rate which is paid for loans, and if this market is a free competitive market the rate of interest which is paid on call loans will be the result of the relationship which exists between demand and supply.

If any control whatever of the supply of money available for call loans were obtained, the call money rate paid by borrowers would at once cease to be determined entirely by these two factors of supply and demand. In the event that there existed any such control of the funds which supply the money market, a monopoly would result on the side of the lenders of money who had control of this supply of funds for the market. They would in this case be able to regulate the price, in the form of the interest rate, through their limitation of supply. If, on the other hand, there were any control of the demand, this would have to come about through a combination of the borrowers. The borrowers would limit the amount of call loans demanded and hence regulate the interest rate in this way. Unless there were some control on the side either of demand or of supply, there could not be any effective control of the interest rate which is paid for call loans.

The assertion has been frequently made that some control does exist in the New York money market and that the rates charged for call loans are manipulated for the benefit of those who are in control of the market. There have been investigations of the conditions and one of the best known of these was that of the Pujo Committee. This was a Congressional committee which investigated the matter as to whether or not there existed a money trust in New York City. Their conclusions on the subject were somewhat vague. Although they appeared to think that such a trust might exist, they never found that it actually operated. It would seem that if there had been any evidence of such a trust they would not have failed to find it. A study of all the stock transactions and of all the flotations of stock and bond issues should have shown whether or not there was any group of men who had any control of the money market.

A Free Market.—It is the belief of the writer that there is no control in the New York Call Money Market which could have any command over the demand for call loans or which could have any control of the supply of funds and hence the rate of interest paid on such loans. This belief is based upon the following facts:

1. There is no limitation upon borrowers to obtain funds in any one market; there are three independent money markets and the borrower may obtain his loan in any of them. They operate entirely independent of each other and are not organized under the control of any one body.
2. There is no control of the supply of funds which is available for call loans in the money market.
3. The renewal rate as determined by the Stock Clearing Corporation and the Governing Committee of the Stock Exchange is closely followed only in the call money market on the floor of the Stock Exchange, and even here it is not compulsory for either the lenders or the borrowers to accept this rate as determined. Furthermore it is not closely followed by the outside money markets, because in these markets there are many individual agreements between borrowers and lenders as to what the rate shall be.

Each of these three facts has an important bearing upon the discussion as to whether the New York Call Money Market is a free market, in which funds are borrowed and lent without any control of the interest rate, or whether it is a controlled market.

The existence of three distinct money markets, in which borrowers may seek funds, or in which lenders may offer them, gives the lenders no means of controlling the supply of money. Unless this supply can be controlled and the borrower compelled to obtain his funds in one market, where the supply is thus controlled, there is no way of limiting the amount of money which will be invested in call loans. Call loans will compete with other types of investment and banks or other lenders will invest their money wherever they find most advantages in regard to the return and the kind of investment. Even if the renewal rate were compulsory on all lenders and borrowers in the money market on the floor of the Exchange, this could not have any serious effect on the money market as a whole. If the rate were fixed too high, that is to say higher than justified by business and banking conditions, two things would happen. First, borrowers would reduce the amount of their loans in this market and would seek funds outside of the Stock Exchange money market. In the second place, more funds would be sent for investment in stock exchange loans than there would be demand for, with the result that part of these funds would not find investment in the money market. When banks find that their funds remain idle, they would either offer them at a lower rate outside the Exchange, or withdraw them altogether from the call money market.

Whenever the renewal rate is a little off, and not fixed at the figure justified by demand and supply, the fact becomes apparent in the increase of the turnover in loans. This increase in the turnover means that some of the borrowers or lenders are not satisfied with the rate and that they are shifting their loans. Thus, if the rate is too high, there will be a withdrawal of some borrowers who will secure funds elsewhere; on the other hand, if the renewal rate is too low, banks will withdraw part of their funds and lend them either in the outside market, or invest them in something else.

The freedom which lenders have as to the amount of money they shall lend and as to the market in which they shall lend seems to prove conclusively that there is no control over supply. If there existed some limitation upon the amount of funds which outside banks send to New York as deposits and to be loaned in the money market, then some control might be exercised by pressure being put upon the New York banks. But the liberty which out-of-town banks possess as to what amount of money they shall invest in call loans in New York City makes it virtually impossible to exercise any control. New York banks encourage the country banks to send their funds to New York, because of the profits which they make on the balances which the out-of-town banks keep in New York. They pay the country banks a rate of interest which is small enough to allow them to re-lend the money in either call or time loans at a good profit.

Why Country Banks Keep Funds in New York City.—There are several reasons why the country banks find it advantageous to keep funds in New York banks. First, the country bank wishes to be able to sell drafts on New York for the accommodation of its customers who may desire to remit drafts of payment. A second reason is that the country bank desires to have agents in New York to handle and collect drafts drawn by dealers or manufacturers of its locality who have shipped goods to distant markets. Further the country bank must have collection agencies for the stream of checks deposited daily by its customers. Another reason worthy of note is that it allows the country banks to lend funds on the New York call money market. This uncontrolled amount of out-of-town money plays a large part in the money market as will be shown later, and the New York banks blame the country banks for a great part of their financial troubles, which they claim are the result of sudden withdrawals by the country banks of their support of the money market.

On the demand side there is an absence of any control which is exercised as to the amount which may be borrowed by any broker provided he has the necessary collateral to put up on his borrowings, and provided this collateral is satisfactory to the lender. Naturally, there is a limitation upon the amount of funds which brokers can secure upon their personal credit, but there is no limitation upon the amount of call loans which may be secured with satisfactory collateral.

There was one period in the history of the New York Call Money Market when it was under control, and that was during the supervision of the Money Committee. This period was discussed in the last chapter, and it is evident that in order to exercise any effective control the Money Committee found it necessary to be able to literally "peg" the market. That is to say, the supply of funds was fixed and the demand for these funds was also fixed by the provision that no broker should increase the amount of his loans above a certain predetermined figure. There was no advantage in bidding large rates of interest because a certain amount of money was guaranteed, and no more was allowed under any conditions. With this control of demand and supply the Money Committee had complete control of the money market for call loans. They were able to control the interest rates on call loans through this control of the forces of demand and supply.

Is Control Desirable?—It might be urged that some control of the money market would be desirable. As to that it may here be stated that there would be certain advantages which would result from such control, but whether or not it would be tolerated in normal times is doubtful. It was a very good war measure and the result was that call money rates did not get above seven per cent during the whole time that the Money Committee was in control. If there had been no control rates would undoubtedly have gone very much higher, in spite of the credit facilities of the Federal Reserve System. This was shown by the fact that after control was relinquished by the Money Committee, rates went to fifteen per cent and even to thirty per cent for a day in November 1919.

Although the Federal Reserve System greatly lessened the financial strain in the money market, it should be remembered that a very important part was played by the Money Committee, and that it was this committee which kept the New York Call Money Market in control.

There are a great many arguments against any such control in normal times. Although it would lessen the probability of any crises occurring in the stock market, and minimize financial strain, it would limit the market more than would be advisable if the same methods were used as during the last period of control. It will be remembered that there was an insistent demand upon the part of brokers and bankers alike that the supervision of the money market should be done away with after the necessity for it as a war measure was no longer urgent. Any strict limitation would have a discouraging effect upon industrial expansion in all probability. In floating new issues, corporations depend to a very great extent upon the money market, and they attempt to make these flotations at times when there appears to be a boom in business or when there are surplus funds seeking investment. If somebody had control of the supply of funds and could tell the corporations when and how they might be able to make new issues, then the control of this body would indeed be too powerful to be tolerated.

There would be a large amount of jealousy and suspicion attached to any person or any group who had control of the market. It would be maintained that this group manipulated the money market for the purpose of furthering their own interests. Changes in the condition of the New York Call Money Market are often reflected in the securities which are more or less speculative in character, or in the prices of any securities in which there is some speculation going on. A rise in the rate charged for call loans often brings about a drop in those stocks which are bought for speculation and most of which are held on margin. The reason for this is that the rate of interest is a very large factor in the profits of the speculator. He must borrow a large proportion of the money he uses to buy the securities, and if he must pay a higher rate of interest on this money the securities must rise that much higher in price before he is able to realize any profits. For example, if a man buys, on margin, one hundred shares of stock at one hundred dollars a share, he will put up money to the sum of perhaps two thousand dollars and he will have to pay interest upon the other eight thousand dollars which the broker has borrowed for him in order to carry the stock. It is evident that any increase in the rate of interest will cause the speculator some trepidation, and he will profit, only if the stock goes up high enough to pay him sufficiently. On the other hand, a decrease in the call money rate has a tendency to stimulate speculative activity because of the lower cost of carrying securities on margin. There is some difference between the result on the stock market of a rise in the interest rates on call loans, and a fall in these rates in relation to the time which it takes for the result to become apparent. An increase in the rate may have an almost immediate reflection in the stock prices, and will generally affect those, in which there is some speculation, the most heavily, whereas a fall in the call money rate may have no immediate effect. The reason why this is likely to happen is obvious. When the money is invested, then the speculators may begin to withdraw at the first sign of a weakening market and the difficulties which attend an increase in the call money rate, but they will not be so eager always to enter into the purchase of stocks, even if the call money rate drops.

On account of the connection which exists between the New York Stock Exchange and the call money market, it is doubtful if any person or group of persons could possibly be found that would be free from criticism and suspicion if they had control of the money market. It would be almost impossible for anyone in possession of such power not to exercise it in favoring his own interests. It would hardly seem likely that the power would be used contrary to the interests of those in control, whether it be a body representative of the banking interests or of the United States Government. The fixing of the renewal rate is entirely justifiable and is of assistance in calculating the condition of the money market, but the control of demand and supply would probably never be tolerated except in such periods as the World War.

Supply of Funds as Affected by the Federal Reserve System.—The New York money market and the security collateral loan occupy a somewhat different place in the eyes of bankers since the inauguration of the Federal Reserve System. This is especially true in the case of out-of-town bankers. One of the purposes of the Federal Reserve Act was to lessen the dependence of the out-of-town banks upon the New York money market for the investment of their secondary reserves. One of the provisions of the Act was that no deposits in New York banks would be allowed to be counted as reserves of country banks. Under the National Banking Law the reserve requirements were as follows:

1. Country banks, 15 per cent, of which three-fifths might be deposited in a bank in a reserve city.
2. Reserve city banks, 25 per cent, of which one-half might be deposited in a bank in a central reserve city (New York, Chicago, St. Louis).
3. Central reserve city banks, 25 per cent in their own vaults.

The central reserve cities had to have a population of 200,000, and reserve cities 25,000. The result of this law was that there were about 60 reserve cities in which the country banks could deposit their reserves, and that there were three central reserve cities in which these reserve cities could deposit their reserves. The result of this law was that a large part of the reserves of the banks all over the country found their way to the New York banks where a great proportion of them were loaned in the call money market. Furthermore the country banks were accustomed to send a large amount of funds other than their reserves to New York to be loaned on the call money market. As a result, in times when the country banks had very little use for their funds at home, these funds were sent to New York, where they were either invested in call loans or put on deposit at the New York banks to draw the low rate of interest paid by the New York banks which in their turn sought investment for these funds.

There was, consequently, at times a great surplus of money in New York which was available for an expansion of credit. The low rates which prevailed during these periods fostered speculative activity, which gradually absorbed most of these funds at interest rates which would tend to rise as the speculative movement got under way. Then, at this period of the business cycle, the trouble started because of the fact that the country banks would wish to withdraw some of their money from New York. With the growth of business activity the out-of-town banks would find that they had use of their funds at home. Their own customers would make demands on them for increases of credit and then these banks would call on New York to send back part of the money which was held for them in New York. Or there might be a sudden tightening of money and the country banks would get panicky and demand their funds from New York. As a result of this state of affairs there would be sharp increases in call money rates and sometimes a crisis or even a panic. This method of banking under the National Banking Act was considered to be one of the main causes of those painful convulsions in business to which our country has been periodically subjected. Wesley Mitchell has shown very clearly in his book "Business Cycles" * how the fluctuations in the supply of credit affected the rate of interest charged for call loans, with the result that we have records of rates anywhere from 0 to 186 per cent. All of the surplus funds and reserves of the banks of the country were massed in New York City.

Federal Reserve Act and New York Money Market.—The Federal Reserve Act attempted to alleviate this state of affairs. In the first place the reserves of all national banks must be kept in the form of credits with a federal reserve bank. The ratios which must be kept in the Federal reserve bank are:

1. Country banks 7 per cent against all demand deposits.
2. Reserve cities 10 per cent against all demand deposits.
3. Central reserve cities 13 per cent against all demand deposits.
4. Federal reserve banks must keep 35 per cent against these deposits in gold in their own vaults.

In this way the reserves of the banks throughout the country were concentrated in the twelve federal reserve banks, and not in New York City. After attending to this matter of the reserves of the country

* Wesley Mitchell: Business Cycles. 1911.

banks, and also those of other cities, the next point for the framers of the Federal Reserve Act to settle was how the funds of these banks were to be invested. Some substitute was to be made for the New York Call Money Market.

The Federal Reserve System then inaugurated a discount market in order to give the country banks some other means of investing their funds rather than depending entirely upon the call loan. It was thought that if a broad market for commercial paper could be built up, so that country banks could invest their surplus funds in the purchase of this paper rather than in the call loan, the evil would be to a great extent eliminated. The division of the banking system into twelve separate districts was to bring about a decrease in the amount of business done through the New York banks and the dependence of the out-of-town banks on New York by three means: The reserve requirements, the discount market, and the check collection system.

It was hoped that the Federal Reserve System would decrease the amount of deposits in the New York banks, and the loans for the account of correspondents more than has been the case. There are several reasons why the out-of-town banks still find it to their advantage to keep a certain amount of their deposits and surplus funds in New York City.

Continued Placement of Out-of-Town Funds on Money Market.—In the first place, lending money on the New York money market is about the easiest way imaginable for out-of-town banks to lend their funds. Take, for example, a country banker who has $25,000 which he wishes to invest in a liquid form of investment. If he invests this money in the money market he has merely to telegraph his New York correspondent to lend $25,000 for him on the New York Call Money Market. All the work which is attached to the placing of the loan is done by the New York bank with the help of the brokers, and the country banker has merely to send the telegram. If the same banker wished to invest this same amount of money in acceptances, he would be compelled to go out and buy the acceptances and get them in such denominations that they would amount to the sum of money he wished to invest. He would have more work to do in connection with the making of the loan, such as scrutinizing the paper, obtaining acceptances or bills of the desired maturity, and all other details. It is, furthermore, equally easy for the country banker to reduce the amount of his loans on the New York call money market. In the event that he wishes to withdraw funds, he telegraphs his correspondent in New York to call loans which are placed for him to the amount which he wishes to withdraw. It is immaterial to the country banker how this is done; all he knows is that he telegraphs and gets his money.

Another reason which sometimes operates to encourage the country banker to make use of the call loan is the fact that the rate of interest paid upon call loans is at times higher than the contemporary rate which may be had in the acceptance market. It cannot be said that the rate on call loans is always higher than that on acceptances, but this is ordinarily the case except in a very easy market. The difference is generally between one-half and one per cent.

The third reason for the preference of the banker of the New York money market is on account of the fact that the New York market is a much broader one than any acceptance market in the United States. Theoretically, there should exist twelve acceptance markets, one in each bank district of the Federal Reserve System, but practically there is no large development of the discount market in most of the districts. Their banking business is not such as lends itself to the use of acceptances. Agriculture will not have much business which will result in acceptances, nor the lumber business, nor many others which are very important in this country. Country bankers realize that the small individual loans which they make in the call money market are practically negligible in comparison with the huge volume of funds which is daily lent or withdrawn from the market. Hence they feel no trepidation as to what effect their withdrawals will have on such a market, whereas in a more limited and narrow market similar withdrawals, would have a serious effect on the general tone of the market from which they were withdrawn. If there were one great acceptance market for the whole country, instead of the twelve which now are supposed to exist, there would be more chance of successfully developing such a market.

There is no personal element in loans made upon the New York Call Money Market. The borrower does not know from what bank outside the city the funds originally came, and the country banker does not know to whom his funds have been loaned. Thus no personal ill-feeling is created on either side by the calling of loans. If a loan is called and the borrower is unable to pay it, his securities may be immediately sold in order to secure the amount of the loan.

Attempts are being made to bring the country bankers to the point of investing in the bill market by means of educating them as to what that market is and what place it holds in the economic organization of the country. Also there has been much done to encourage business men to make use of trade acceptances which are eligible for rediscount with the federal reserve banks. Whether or not these attempts will be rewarded with any large success remains to be seen; but it is undoubtedly a hard task to turn the country bankers away from a type of investment which they consider so liquid and safe as the call loan. Some of the country banks are not even members of the Federal Reserve System and some of the bankers do not know what the acceptance market is. These things make the increased and widespread use of the acceptance doubly difficult. Some bankers do business the way it has always been done by their forerunners, and, in their eyes, what was good enough for their fathers is good enough for them. Until they can be shown some positive advantages accruing to themselves as a result of investing funds in the acceptance market, it is probable that they will continue to use the New York Call Money Market for the purpose of investing their temporarily idle funds. In those districts in which there have been numerous bank failures, such as the North-west, some of the soundest banks have a large proportion of their funds invested in the form of call loans in New York. They are in this way independent of the condition of the banks of their district to a much larger extent than would be the case if they had large holdings of obligations of the banks of their locality.

Comparison of Call Money Rates under National Banking System and under Federal Reserve System. —Although it is doubtful whether there has been any considerable decrease in the amount of out-of-town money which is loaned in the New York Call Money Market, still it is true that the rates of interest charged on these loans have varied far less under the Federal Reserve System than they did under the National Banking Act. It is also undoubtedly true that there has been far less seasonal variation in the volume of out-of-town money since the inauguration of our new banking system. One of the principal reasons why there has been less variation in the call money rates has been the greatly increased credit facilities of the Federal Reserve System in comparison with those facilities which formerly existed. When the call money rate increases until it reaches a level which is considerably higher than the federal reserve discount rate, an effort is made by banks to discount more paper with the federal reserve bank and lend the proceeds on this borrowing, on the money market. In this way the increased demand of the borrower is met to a great extent and the call money rate is kept within reasonable limits. Then if the federal reserve bank wishes to discourage the increase in credit, the discount rate is raised. In this way there is a more gradual deflation of the loans than was the case under the national banking system where credit generally remained easy to obtain until the banks had almost reached the end of their lending power, with the result that they found it necessary to make a sudden halt in the extension of credit with disastrous results for the money market.

The lower limits of call money rates are determined by the rate of interest which may be earned by investing funds in similar types of liquid obligations, such as bankers' acceptances and other forms of investment which have already been discussed.

Table I below, and the accompanying chart, Figure I, show the relative variations which have taken place in the call money rate under the National Banking System and under the Federal Reserve System. The rates on call loans under the National Banking System are the average weekly rates as computed by Professor Kemmerer in his work "Seasonal Variations in the Relative Demand for Money and Capital in the

United States."* They cover the years 1890-1908. The rate of interest on call loans since the inauguration of the Federal Reserve System are the average weekly rates computed from those given in the Commercial and Financial Chronicle.

TABLE I. AVERAGE WEEKLY CALL MONEY RATES UNDER THE NATIONAL BANKING SYSTEM AND THE FEDERAL RESERVE SYSTEM

		N. B. S.	F. R. S.			N. B. S.	F. R. S.
Jan.	1	6.42	5.21	July	27	3.42	4.67
	2	3.62	3.99		28	2.92	4.90
	3	2.84	4.09		29	2.30	4.89
	4	2.50	3.44		30	2.37	4.15
Feb.	5	2.45	4.13	Aug.	31	2.45	3.78
	6	2.39	4.94		32	2.54	3.76
	7	2.54	4.35		33	2.64	4.12
	8	2.70	3.85		34	3.66	3.76
Mar.	9	2.97	4.25	Sept.	35	3.04	4.69
	10	2.58	4.24		36	4.13	4.86
	11	3.85	3.81		37	4.16	4.76
	12	3.24	3.68		38	4.33	4.87
Apr.	13	3.62	4.16		39	4.23	5.29
	14	4.00	3.91	Oct.	40	4.48	5.33
	15	3.78	3.96		41	3.97	5.39
	16	3.03	4.01		42	3.56	4.89
	17	2.94	4.04		43	6.53	5.56
May	18	3.37	4.18	Nov.	44	7.08	5.69
	19	3.47	4.26		45	5.44	5.91
	20	2.64	4.01		46	4.80	5.06
	21	2.44	3.94		47	4.25	4.91
June	22	2.28	4.66	Dec.	48	3.95	4.84
	23	2.31	4.59		49	4.85	5.06
	24	2.41	4.90		50	5.49	4.91
	25	2.51	5.01		51	6.64	4.98
July	26	3.56	4.55		52	7.38	5.01

* Kemmerer: Seasonal Variations in the Relative Demand for Money and Capital in the United States. 1905.

From these figures and the chart it is obvious that the call money rate has varied less since the beginning of the Federal Reserve System than was the case formerly. It should be kept in mind, however, that the period under which the Federal Reserve System

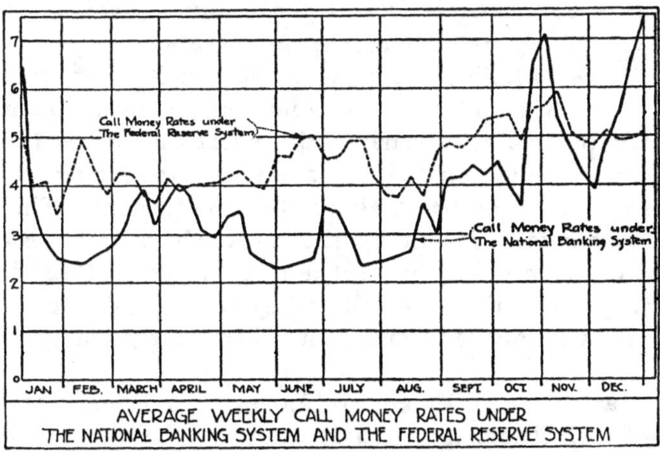

Figure 1.

has been operated is not a period of anywhere near normal conditions. There was little chance for the new banking system to get into operation before the World War; then for a period of about two years the Money Committee had control of the money market; after this period, the country went through a severe economic crisis. As a result, there has been little chance as yet to see just what the seasonal fluctuations in the call money rate will be, and just how the Federal Reserve System will show its influence upon these money rates. Professor Kemmerer has worked out some very interesting seasonal variations as they operated under the first period in the history of the New York Call Money Market, but as yet no such work seems possible for the period during which our new banking system has been in operation.

It seems highly probable that the call money rate will vary less under normal conditions, or over a long period of time, than it has in this short time under the abnormal conditions which have existed so far during the operation of the Federal Reserve System. This judgment is born out by the rates which have prevailed in the money market during the years 1922-23, during which time the call money rate has shown no large variations, and money has been fairly plentiful.

Variations in Volume of Loans, and Effect upon the Stock Exchange.—An attempt will here be made to estimate the effect which variations in the volume of call loans have upon the transactions which take place on the New York Stock Exchange. As there are no limitations upon the amount of money which may be borrowed or loaned, the volume of this money loaned in proportion to the total demand for it will determine the call money rate. Figures are not available for the total demand for call loans, but a very large part of this demand is in connection with the New York Stock Exchange where securities are bought, sold, and held by means of these call loans. In this discussion four different factors will be considered in their mutual relationship; the call money rate, the volume of loans, the volume of transactions, and the price of securities. The first two of these factors give a picture of the conditions which exist in the money market, while the latter two show the conditions which exist on the Stock Exchange. It remains to see what the relationship is between these different factors. Naturally they must be somewhat inter-related, but the question is, what happens when money is withdrawn or brought into the money market, and, furthermore, what effect does the call money rate actually have upon the volume of money offered? Also what effect does the price of securities and volume of securities have on the money market?

The period used in the chart which is given (Figure 2) is necessarily a rather short one, because of the fact that figures are not ordinarily available as to what the volume of loans is; consequently, that period must be used in which we have figures for this factor. This period begins January 1919, and ends July 1921; the figures for the volume of loans were made public in the testimony of Governor Strong of the New York Federal Reserve Bank in connection with the Agricultural Inquiry. The call money rate during this period is taken from the "Commercial and Financial Chronicle." The index of stock prices is that of industrial stocks during this period. The tables for these four different groups of figures are given below, accompanied by a chart of the four curves. (Figure 2.)

TABLE 2. VOLUME OF LOANS [DATES COVERED] JANUARY 1919—JULY 1921

(000,000 omitted)

Date	Loans for Account of Correspondents	Loans for Own Account	Total Loans
1919			
Jan. 3	219	574	794
Jan. 10	232	542	774
Jan. 17	250	530	780
Jan. 24	243	532	776
Jan. 31	237	539	777
Feb. 7	241	531	773
Feb. 14	241	531	773
Feb. 21	259	513	772
Feb. 28	263	529	793
Mar. 7	290	512	792
Mar. 14	290	530	821
Mar. 21	290	540	830
Mar. 28	304	556	860
Apr. 4	300	559	860
Apr. 11	295	604	900
Apr. 18	319	624	944
Apr. 25	339	628	967
May 2	367	629	996
May 9	371	650	1,022
May 16	383	679	1,062
May 23	414	692	1,107
May 29	408	738	1,146
June 6	455	750	1,205
June 13	466	771	1,238
June 20	477	750	1,228
June 27	478	768	1,246
July 3	493	771	1,264
July 11	436	770	1,306
July 18	569	797	1,366
July 25	578	758	1,337
Aug. 1	588	795	1,385

Date	Loans for Account of Correspondents	Loans for Own Account	Total Loans
1919			
Aug. 8	601	766	1,367
Aug. 15	590	740	1,331
Aug. 22	557	720	1,282
Aug. 29	575	690	1,266
Sept. 5	580	709	1,290
Sept. 12	594	698	1,294
Sept. 19	581	719	1,301
Sept. 26	577	735	1,313
Oct. 3	583	771	1,355
Oct. 10	612	763	1,376
Oct. 17	650	766	1,417
Oct. 24	666	784	1,451
Oct. 31	689	821	1,511
Nov. 7	736	781	1,518
Nov. 14	735	687	1,422
Nov. 21	740	627	1,368
Nov. 28	725	633	1,359
Dec. 5	716	595	1,312
Dec. 12	677	630	1,308
Dec. 19	657	641	1,298
Dec. 26	639	662	1,302
1920			
Jan. 2	634	714	1,349
Jan. 9	670	694	1,364
Jan. 16	681	640	1,322
Jan. 23	677	624	1,302
Jan. 30	374	606	1,280
Feb. 6	681	556	1,237
Feb. 13	669	484	1,154
Feb. 20	649	444	1,094
Feb. 27	648	442	1,091
Mar. 5	638	435	1,073
Mar. 12	625	450	1,076
Mar. 19	636	452	1,088
Mar. 26	621	459	1,080
Apr. 2	611	475	1,087
Apr. 9	627	461	1,088
Apr. 16	631	491	1,123
Apr. 23	637	468	1,106
Apr. 30	603	484	1,088

Date	Loans for Account of Correspondents	Loans for Own Account	Total Loans
1920			
May 7	612	451	1,064
May 14	595	424	1,019
May 21	582	422	1,005
May 28	549	420	970
June 4	525	419	944
June 11	518	412	931
June 18	522	429	952
June 25	506	437	944
July 2	501	436	938
July 9	527	419	946
July 16	519	404	923
July 23	530	386	916
July 30	533	379	912
Aug. 6	530	354	885
Aug. 13	525	337	863
Aug. 20	533	346	879
Aug. 27	513	348	862
Sept. 3	513	329	843
Sept. 10	527	344	871
Sept. 17	540	341	881
Sept. 24	529	346	875
Oct. 1	522	373	895
Oct. 15	535	437	973
Oct. 22	549	400	949
Oct. 29	559	393	952
Nov. 5	573	380	954
Nov. 12	589	346	935
Nov. 19	560	326	887
Nov. 26	521	326	848
Dec. 3	514	337	820
Dec. 10	516	346	863
Dec. 17	485	352	838
Dec. 24	441	365	807
Dec. 31	426	387	813
1921			
Jan. 2	439	346	785
Jan. 14	445	335	780
Jan. 21	445	356	802
Jan. 28	431	340	772
Feb. 4	438	344	782

Date	Loans for Account of Correspondents	Loans for Own Account	Total Loans
1921			
Feb. 11	456	312	769
Feb. 18	463	313	777
Feb. 25	450	331	782
Mar. 4	458	334	793
Mar. 11	463	319	783
Mar. 18	459	312	771
Mar. 25	451	313	765
Apr. 1	436	320	757
Apr. 8	425	325	751
Apr. 15	427	317	774
Apr. 22	440	307	748
Apr. 29	440	323	763
May 4	447	307	754
May 11	461	309	770
May 18	460	320	781
May 25	456	328	784
June 1	434	358	793
June 8	472	313	786
June 15	457	338	796
June 22	422	331	754
June 29	395	348	743
July 6	384	339	724
July 13	408	332	741
July 20	393	346	739

TABLE 3. CALL MONEY RATE [DATES COVERED] JANUARY 1919—JULY 1921

Date	Rate	Date	Rate	Date	Rate
1919		Feb. 21	5.00	Apr. 25	5.00
		Feb. 28	5.75	May 2	5.75
Jan. 3	6.00	Mar. 7	4.75	May 9	5.00
Jan. 10	5.00	Mar. 14	4.75	May 16	5.50
Jan. 17	4.50	Mar. 21	4.75	May 23	5.50
Jan. 24	4.50	Mar. 28	5.25	May 29	5.00
Jan. 31	4.50	Apr. 4	5.00	June 6	6.25
Feb. 7	4.50	Apr. 11	5.50	June 13	6.25
Feb. 14	5.00	Apr. 18	5.75	June 20	8.00

Date	Rate
1919	
June 27	7.00
July 3	7.25
July 11	7.10
July 18	6.50
July 25	6.40
Aug. 1	7.00
Aug. 8	5.40
Aug. 15	6.25
Aug. 22	4.75
Aug. 29	5.50
Sept. 5	5.75
Sept. 12	4.75
Sept. 19	6.00
Sept. 26	8.00
Oct. 3	8.50
Oct. 10	9.25
Oct. 17	5.50
Oct. 24	8.50
Oct. 31	11.50
Nov. 7	15.00
Nov. 14	10.50
Nov. 21	7.25
Nov. 28	6.25
Dec. 5	8.00
Dec. 12	6.50
Dec. 19	8.00
Dec. 26	9.75
1920	
Jan. 2	13.75
Jan. 9	7.00
Jan. 16	8.75
Jan. 23	6.50
Jan. 30	9.00
Feb. 6	15.25
Feb. 13	9.75
Feb. 20	6.50
Feb. 27	8.25
Mar. 5	9.50
Mar. 12	7.25
Mar. 19	7.75
Mar. 26	7.75
Apr. 2	8.00
Apr. 9	6.25
Apr. 16	7.50
Apr. 23	7.50
Apr. 30	7.50
May 7	7.50
May 14	7.00
May 21	6.00
May 28	10.00
June 4	7.50
June 11	9.50
June 18	10.00
June 25	8.50
July 2	9.00
July 9	8.50
July 16	8.50
July 23	7.00
July 30	6.50
Aug. 6	8.00
Aug. 13	8.50
Aug. 20	7.00
Aug. 27	7.00
Sept. 3	6.50
Sept. 10	7.00
Sept. 17	8.00
Sept. 24	7.50
Oct. 1	8.00
Oct. 8	7.50
Oct. 15	9.00
Oct. 22	9.50
Oct. 29	8.50
Nov. 5	7.50
Nov. 12	6.00
Nov. 19	6.50
Nov. 26	7.00
Dec. 3	7.00
Dec. 10	6.75
Dec. 17	6.50
Dec. 24	7.00
Dec. 31	7.00
1921	
Jan. 7	7.00
Jan. 14	6.50
Jan. 21	6.25
Jan. 28	7.00
Feb. 4	7.50
Feb. 11	7.00
Feb. 18	7.00
Feb. 25	7.00
Mar. 4	7.00
Mar. 11	7.00
Mar. 18	7.00
Mar. 25	6.50
Apr. 1	6.50
Apr. 8	6.00
Apr. 15	6.75
Apr. 22	6.50
Apr. 29	6.50
May 4	6.75
May 11	6.50
May 18	7.00
May 25	7.00
June 1	7.10
June 8	7.00
June 15	5.75
June 22	5.00
June 29	5.50
July 6	5.50
July 13	5.75
July 20	6.00

TABLE 4. VOLUME OF STOCK EXCHANGE TRANSACTIONS [DATES COVERED] JANUARY 1919—JULY 1921

(000,000 omitted)

Date	Amount	Date	Amount	Date	Amount
1919		Sept. 13	458	May 22	369
Jan. 14	359	Sept. 20	413	May 29	309
Jan. 11	242	Sept. 27	465	June 5	244
Jan. 18	238	Oct. 4	729	June 12	211
Jan. 25	284	Oct. 11	707	June 19	203
Feb. 1	244	Oct. 18	584	June 26	168
Feb. 8	186	Oct. 25	897	July 3	162
Feb. 15	182	Nov. 1	776	July 10	405
Feb. 22	394	Nov. 8	664	July 17	285
Mar. 1	386	Nov. 15	964	July 24	156
Mar. 8	413	Nov. 22	624	July 31	295
Mar. 15	597	Nov. 29	444	Aug. 7	433
Mar. 22	561	Dec. 6	502	Aug. 14	256
Mar. 29	322	Dec. 13	506	Aug. 21	170
Apr. 5	431	Dec. 20	484	Aug. 28	237
Apr. 12	643	Dec. 27	354	Sept. 4	267
Apr. 19	481	1920		Sept. 11	252
Apr. 26	745	Jan. 3	517	Sept. 18	251
May 3	813	Jan. 10	523	Sept. 25	395
May 10	669	Jan. 17	505	Oct. 2	411
May 17	829	Jan. 24	290	Oct. 9	401
May 24	725	Jan. 31	318	Oct. 16	257
May 31	710	Feb. 6	579	Oct. 23	215
June 7	800	Feb. 13	517	Oct. 30	252
June 14	763	Feb. 21	461	Nov. 6	334
June 21	654	Feb. 28	526	Nov. 13	556
June 28	632	Mar. 6	350	Nov. 20	530
July 5	546	Mar. 13	653	Nov. 27	353
July 11	725	Mar. 20	645	Dec. 4	356
July 19	842	Mar. 27	706	Dec. 11	397
July 26	650	Apr. 3	320	Dec. 18	459
Aug. 2	513	Apr. 10	595	Dec. 25	513
Aug. 9	781	Apr. 17	588	1921	
Aug. 16	453	Apr. 24	786	Jan. 1	408
Aug. 23	463	May 1	511	Jan. 8	342
Aug. 30	379	May 8	373	Jan. 15	417
Sept. 6	790	May 15	358	Jan. 22	281

Date	Amount	Date	Amount	Date	Amount
1921		Mar. 26	252	May 28	423
		Apr. 2	262	June 4	153
Jan. 29	231	Apr. 9	193	June 11	305
Feb. 5	219	Apr. 16	218	June 18	354
Feb. 12	188	Apr. 23	197	June 25	365
Feb. 19	233	Apr. 30	368	July 2	255
Feb. 26	157	May 7	393	July 9	220
Mar. 5	208	May 14	336	July 16	169
Mar. 12	243	May 21	242	July 23	127
Mar. 19	303				

TABLE 5. INDEX PRICE OF STOCKS [DATES COVERED] JANUARY 1919—JULY 1921

Date	Price	Date	Price	Date	Price
1919		Dec.	107.97	Nov.	85.48
		1920		Dec.	77.63
Jan.	83.35			1921	
Feb.	85.68	Jan.	109.88		
Mar.	89.05	Feb.	103.01	Jan.	76.76
Apr.	93.51	Mar.	104.17	Feb.	77.14
May	105.50	Apr.	105.65	Mar.	77.78
June	107.55	May	94.75	Apr.	78.86
July	112.23	June	93.20	May	80.03
Aug.	107.09	July	94.51	June	73.51
Sept.	111.42	Aug.	87.29	July	69.86
Oct.	118.92	Sept.	89.95		
Nov.	119.62	Oct.	85.73		

When the chart in Figure 2 is examined, one observes that during the first six months there was a decided rise in three of the four curves, namely: The volume of loans, the volume of transactions, and the price of stocks. One of the most powerful causes of this rise was the fact that the money market and the New York Stock Exchange became free of all supervision by the Money Committee in January

Graph of Call Money Rates, Volume of Loans, Volume of Security Transactions, and Stock Prices, from January 1919 to July 1921
KEY
Total Loans
Call Money Rate
Total Stock Transactions
N.Y. Stock Prices
Total Stock Transactions - Millions of Dollars
Total Loans - Hundreds of Thousands of Dollars
Call Money Rate - Percent
Stock Prices
YEAR 1919
YEAR 1920
YEAR 1921

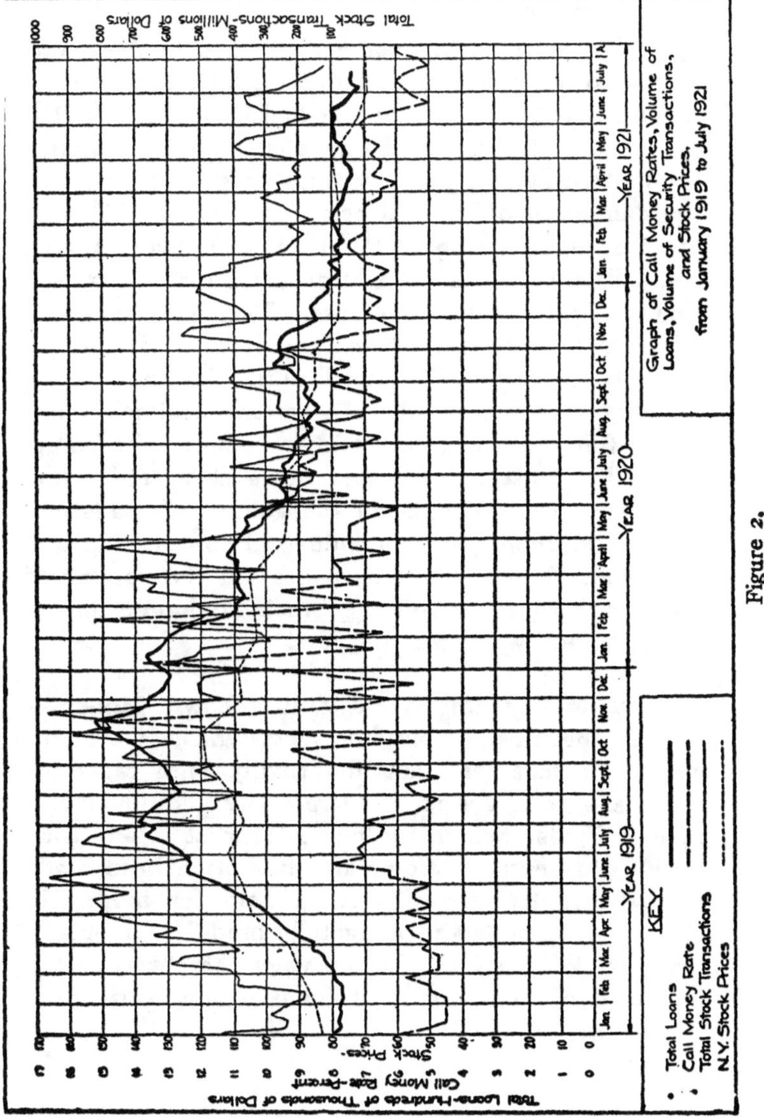

Figure 2.

1919. After the relinquishment of control there was a great reaction and a period of expansion and speculation started in full force. It had been thought that it was safe to terminate the control of the Money Committee at this time, because of the opinion that the danger of a financial crisis had passed. During the ensuing six months the volume of loans almost doubled and the volume of transactions shows a continual, if intermittent, increase. The price of industrial stocks rose almost forty points. The rise in these three curves continued until November 1919, although the volume of transactions declined for a short time during the summer months preceding. Toward the last of November, however, a break came and there was a decline in the volume of loans and also in the index price of industrial stocks; this was accompanied by a very sharp drop in the volume of the securities traded on the Stock Exchange during the last four weeks of the year.

Call Money Rates and Out-of-Town Money.— One of the most remarkable facts which is brought out in the chart is that abnormally high rates for call loans do not seem to attract any additional volume of funds back to the money market at any time during this period. Complaint has often been made that the high rates of interest paid for money in New York resulted in attracting funds from out-of-town banks, even at periods when there was pressing need of these funds at home. The Agriculturists, for example, claim that they are unable to secure the necessary funds because of the high rates of interest which are paid in New York on the money market; that they are not able to compete with these high New York rates. These claims are not borne out by the figures here given. During the period under consideration, the volume of loans showed its greatest increase at a time when the rates for call money were not at all high, but averaged only about six per cent. This increase in the volume of loans lasted from the first part of 1919 down to the latter part of November of the same year. At the end of this period a general withdrawal of funds took place. Money was tight and the out-of-town banks reduced the amount of money which they had invested in the money market during the previous period when they had no immediate use for their funds.

These out-of-town funds were probably withdrawn for the purpose of strengthening the reserve position of these country banks, in order that they would be better able to satisfy the needs of their own customers. An immediate consequence of this was that the supply fell far short of the demand which had been built up; thus call money rates were very sharply advanced, and for a brief period went as high as fifteen per cent. The call money demand is highly inelastic and a slight shortage of funds will at times cause a large advance in the rates. It would be natural to expect that these high rates would attract some funds back to the New York call money market from outside of the city, but such was not the case. On the contrary, the withdrawals continued with almost unabated speed. This seems to prove that the claims of those agriculturists who complained of the competition of the New York market do not hold good, at least for the period which we are considering.

The reason why the volume does not increase even when the rate of interest is doubled, is that the supply of money available for the New York money market is highly inelastic, and likewise the demand for the funds. Country banks are accustomed to lend a certain amount of their funds, which they desire to keep in a highly liquid form, on the money market in New York City. These funds are composed in most cases, of the surplus funds of the country banks. High money rates on call loans will not tempt the out-of-town banks to lend more money on the money market than they can conveniently afford in accordance with their other demands for money. Furthermore, the country banks know that if funds are sent to New York there is a strong chance that the high money rates will be as quickly lowered as they were raised, because of the inelastic nature of the demand for call loans. A million dollars too small an amount available for the market may cause rates to soar, while a million dollars too large an amount available may put the call money rates far down again. It seems to be true that the out-of-town banks attend first to their local needs for credit, and afterward send funds to New York to be loaned in call loans.

It is sometimes said that the country banks are fearful of loaning money in New York at times when the call money rate is high, because there is a greater risk. It does not appear to the writer that there is much foundation for this reasoning. It would be nearer the truth to say that the country banks either have not the funds available, or that they do not expect that the high rates will last very long. Country banks are always able to get their money back from New York when they need it, in spite of the fact that the New York Stock Exchange was at one time closed, and that these loans became "frozen loans." This happened only once in the history of the Exchange and it is not likely to happen again. The main cause of the closing of the Exchange was that the United States, at the outbreak of the World War, was a debtor nation to Europe, and it was feared that all the securities owned by these nations would be dumped upon the American market. It is hardly likely that anything of this sort will happen again, as this country seems to have assumed the rôle of a creditor nation for many years to come. Whereas we formerly had large remittances to make to Europe every year in the form of interest on loans, dividends on stocks held there, payment for cargoes shipped in foreign bottoms and immigrants' wages, all this is now largely changed and the invisible trade balance against us no longer exists.

There is one very interesting fact in regard to the loans of country banks, which is brought out by the table of figures giving the loans made by New York banks upon the stock exchange and loans made for their correspondents. It appears that there is a decrease in the amount of loans made by the New York banks a week or so before any corresponding decrease takes place in the total volume of loans placed for the account of correspondents. The obvious deduction from this would be that the money market was supported longer in time of tight money by the country banks than by those which one would naturally expect to give financial aid during these periods. Although a reduction in the loan account of the New York banks does take place first, this reduction might be caused to a great extent by the fact that the country banks skin down their balances in the event that they need the money when the call money rate is high, and leave these funds on the money market as long as possible so that they can take advantage of the high rates of interest which prevail at such times. This in turn reduces the lending power of the New York banks. If this took place there would be a reduction in the loan account of the New York banks before any such reduction took place in that of the out-of-town banks. However, it is merely a surmise that this is what takes place and nothing definite can be said in regard to how the phenomenon comes about.

The Call Money Market and Stock Prices.—A study of the chart gives the impression that activity on the New York Stock Exchange and the prices of stocks are far more dependent on the volume of loans than upon the call money rate. The three curves: namely, the volume of loans, the volume of transactions and the price of securities, seem to rise and fall together. The call money rate seems to be the result of the action of these other curves. The call money rate is largely the result of the operation of the forces of demand and supply. The volume of transactions and the prices of securities are here the demand, and the volume of loans is the supply of funds to meet this demand. If these three curves keep the same relation to each other, then the call money rate would not be subject to much variation over short periods of time. Only those variations would take place which were the reflection of the interest rate paid on other investments, which would be the result of the general demand for funds throughout the country and the ability of the supply to meet the demand.

It should be kept in mind that the call money rate is only one of the many factors which determine the course of the stock market, and that there are so many other forces at work that often the effect of a change in the interest rate on call loans is not perceptible. When the market is in a fever of speculation people will be willing to pay high money rates because of the hope which they entertain of making large profits.

If the volume of funds available for the money

market falls behind the demand, there will be a decided rise in the call money rate, and this limitation of the volume of funds must limit the activity of the stock market. It should be remembered, however, that the call money rate only changes with changes in the relationship between demand and supply, and is not fixed independently of these forces. This does not mean that individuals or groups would not be anxious to fix the call rate if it were within their power, but the writer feels that he has shown that such control is not possible.

It is not within the scope of this work to question the ethical considerations involved in the problem of the unearned increment of society in the form of investments, and it is taken for granted that the majority of people are not opposed to the present order of society, socialists and other groups to the contrary notwithstanding. As long as we have these immense amounts of securities in the hands of people all over the country, we should have machinery to move them in case some of these individuals wish to transfer their funds. The New York call money market is necessary to move these funds which are being transferred, and it seems to be the best machinery possible to perform this function. When investors wish to sell securities other investors are not always ready to buy them at the price at which they are selling, and so some one must hold them, or at least a portion of them until an investor is found.

The person who holds them is usually the speculator, who is thus a necessity for the stability of the market, and the call loan is a necessary instrument to provide him with funds to operate.

The New York call money market does not perform its function for the benefit of those in New York City alone, but for investors all over the country who have securities which are listed on the New York Stock Exchange. It is the financial center of the country and the logical place for the financing of corporate enterprise. The call money market, which is a part of the machinery necessary for this financing, is a free market and there exists no centralized control over the demand for or the supply of funds. Anyone is at liberty to lend and borrow money in the market. The call money rate is not a monopoly price which must be paid for call loans, but is a competitive price determined by the law of supply and demand. A study of the call money market does not warrant the conclusion that there is any "money trust" in New York City which controls call money rates; the sources of funds are too varied and numerous. There are large and small lenders, but this is inevitable and a large proportion of the funds is furnished by the small lenders. The ultimate control of all credit must rest in the hands of the Federal Reserve System; but they are definitely able to use this control, which will affect all money rates, only at times when funds are not plentiful in proportion to the demand. At other times the amount of control which they will have over the credit situation in general depends upon the willingness of banks to heed their advice.

INDEX

VITA

Bartow Griffiss was born July 21, 1899, in Pikesville, Maryland.

He received his preparatory education at Marston's University School in Baltimore City, from which he was graduated in 1916. He entered Johns Hopkins University the following fall, and received his Bachelor of Arts degree in the spring of 1920. He started his graduate work in October of that year.

THE UNIVERSITY OF MICHIGAN

UNIVERSITY OF MICHIGAN
3 9015 00404 1334